George F. Bass received his formal academic training in
Near Eastern and classical archaeology. After
participating in conventional digs, he began pioneering
techniques of searching for and excavating underwater
sites, and for ten years directed the University of
Pennsylvania Museum's excavations at Cape Gelidonya
and Yassi Ada in Turkey. Dr Bass is currently
associate professor of classical archaeology at the
University of Pennsylvania and associate curator of
the University Museum's Mediterranean section. He is
a frequent contributor to such publications as
*Antiquity, American Journal of Archaeology, American
Scholar, Archaeology,* and the *National Geographic
Magazine.*

GEORGE F. BASS

ARCHAEOLOGY
UNDER WATER

With 62 photographs, 44 line drawings
and 3 maps

PENGUIN BOOKS

Penguin Books Ltd, Harmondsworth, Middlesex, England
Penguin Books Inc, 7110 Ambassador Road
Baltimore, Maryland 21207, U.S.A.
Penguin Books Australia Ltd, Ringwood, Victoria, Australia

First published in the U.K. by Thames & Hudson 1966
First published in the U.S.A. by Praeger Publishers 1966
Published in Pelican Books 1970

Printed in the United States of America
by Universal Lithographers, Inc
Set in Linotype Juliana

CONTENTS

List of Figures 7

List of Plates 9

Preface 11

1. Introduction 13

2. Working in the Underwater Environment 20

3. Underwater Search and Survey 30

4. Draining and Raising Operations 49

5. The Salvaging of Artifacts 63

6. Mapping and Recording Underwater Sites 82

7. The Tools for Underwater Excavation 110

8. Complete Excavation 132

9. The Future 151

Bibliography 158

Notes on the Plates 167

Index 177

LIST OF FIGURES

1. Scuba diver fully equipped, p. 22
2. Underwater sites in Europe and the Mediterranean, pp. 32–3.
3. Pipes from the Thames, p. 34
4. Underwater sites in North America, p. 37
5. Iron trade axes and chisels, p. 38
6. Effigy censer, p. 40
7. Effigy censer cover, p. 40
8. Underwater sites in Central America and the Caribbean, p. 41
9. The Towvane, p. 46
10. The Vasa being raised, p. 59
11. Pewter powder can, pewter tankard and wooden tankard, from the Vasa, p. 61
12. Early nineteenth-century bottles, p. 64
13. Pipe bowls from a Florida river, p. 64
14. The cenote at Chichen Itza, p. 65
15. South side of the Chichen Itza cenote, p. 66
16. Gilded copper sandal, ear plugs and bracelet from the Chichen Itza cenote, p. 67
17. The cenote at Dzibilchaltun, p. 71
18. Wooden artifacts from the Dzibilchaltun cenote, p. 73
19. Bronze figurine of dwarf from Mahdia, p. 77
20. Bronze herm from Mahdia, p. 78
21. Bronzes from wreck near Béziers, p. 81
22. Plan of wooden piles in the Cambser See, p. 88
23. Cargo of columns near Methone, p. 91
24. Cargo of sarcophagi near Methone, p. 92
25. Method of measuring relative elevations, p. 94
26. Device for measuring curvature of timbers, p. 97

27. Plane table triangulation, *p. 98*

28. Method of measuring relative elevations, *p. 99*

29. Early method for mapping of a wreck, *p. 101*

30. Photo-tower, *p. 102*

31. Method of stereophotographing, *p. 103*

32. Section of the *Asherah*, *p. 106*

33. The *Asherah* mapping a Late Roman wreck, *p. 107*

34. Map of wreck made in a single dive, *p. 108*

35. Scraper and forceps, *p. 112*

36. First use of air lift, *p. 117*

37. Bronze bracelet and pottery bowl, *p. 119*

38. Air lifts used at Cape Gelidonya, *p. 121*

39. Air lift at Yassi Ada, *p. 123*

40. Bronze implements from Cape Gelidonya, *p. 128*

41. Methods used in first season at Yassi Ada, *p. 134*

42. Pottery from cabin area of Byzantine ship, *p. 137*

43. Censer from cabin of Byzantine ship, *p. 138*

44. Methods used in second season at Yassi Ada, *p. 140*

45. Map of visible layer of cargo at Yassi Ada, *p. 141*

46. Rubber casts of tools made from sea concretion moulds, *p. 144*

47. Plan of a fourth-century shipwreck made by photogrammetry, *p. 149*

LIST OF PLATES

1. Diver being got ready for descent
2. Sponge diver inspects cargo of late Roman wreck
3. Four-man recompression chamber
4. Diver jumps into sea with narghile hose
5. Scuba diver battles with rapids
6. Nest of brass and copper kettles
7. Inspecting kettles found in Horsetail Rapids
8. Wooden figure from the stern of the *Vasa*
9. Hollow censer from Lake Amatitlan
10. Effigy censer cover from Lake Amatitlan
11. View of Lake Amatitlan
12. The *Vasa* in dry dock
13. Roman pleasure barge in Lake Nemi
14. The gunboat *Cairo*
15. Air view of coffer dam in Roskilde Fjord, Denmark
16. Stem of a Viking ship in Roskilde Fjord
17. Air lift in the *cenote* at Chichen Itza
18. Gold disc found in the *cenote* at Chichen Itza
19. Bronze god salvaged near Cape Artemision
20. Bronze boy salvaged from Marathon Bay
21. The Piombino Apollo
22. Statue of a youth salvaged near Antikythera
23. Bronze bust of Demeter salvaged near Marmaris
24. Bronze bust of negro youth from Turkish waters
25. Taking underwater measurements from a range pole
26. Diver inspects sunken city of Port Royal, Jamaica
27. Measuring a granite column near Methone
28. Sarcophagi from shipwreck near Methone
29. Underwater telephone booth
30. Differential depth gauge

31. Recording readings of bearing and distance under water
32. Underwater surveying with alidade
33. Rolleimarin camera in use at Yassi Ada
34. Taking elevation measurements of hull fragments from grid
35–6. Stereo-pair of photographs of amphorae
37. Measuring the parallax of stereo-pair
38. The *Asherah* at its naming
39. The *Asherah* diving near Yassi Ada
40. Pair of aerial survey cameras
41. Diver carrying filled air lift bag to surface
42. Air lift ejecting at Port Royal, Jamaica
43. Working at air-lift mouth
44. Divers using air lift on Roman wreck
45. Using underwater metal detector
46. Prospecting with core sampler at Yassi Ada
47. Cutting around concreted cargo with hammer and chisel
48. 3,000-year-old wicker basket found in sea
49. Lifting mass of concreted metal cargo with air balloon
50. Fitting together masses of concreted cargo raised from wreck
51. Sketching brushwood dunnage preserved with Cape Gelidonya wreck
52. Drawing amphorae of Yassi Ada shipwreck *in situ*
53. Using grid for calculating positions of amphorae
54. Methods used in excavating the wreck at Yassi Ada
55. Clearing sand from anchor concretion
56. Cutting concretion with lapidary saw
57. Oil lamps found at Yassi Ada
58. Underwater photograph of wooden plank
59. Bringing up fragile wooden plank in wire basket
60. Reconstructing the plank from fragments
61. Part of the reconstructed plank
62. Submersible decompression chamber

PREFACE

W HEN I was first asked by Dr Glyn Daniel to write a book on archaeology under water, I thought that I should concentrate on the Mediterranean, the area with which I am most familiar. I would like to thank Dr Daniel, and Mr Eric Peters of Thames and Hudson, for encouraging me to include other areas as well, for this has given me the pleasant task of learning much more about the valuable work, past and present, elsewhere in the world.

The figures in the text were drawn mostly by Miss Susan Womer and Mr Eric J. Ryan, both of the diving staff of the Yassi Ada excavations. Miss Womer did all of the object drawings, from photographs or from original artifacts, except for figures 16, 18, and 40, which are credited in their captions; figures 1, 9, and 10 are also by Miss Womer. Mr Ryan drew all of the diagrams and scenes of underwater work except for figures 1, 9, 10, 14, 15, 25b, 26 and 32. Preliminary maps were prepared by Miss Joanna Fink, with the final maps drawn by Mr H. A. Shelley.

A large number of people and institutions have allowed me to reproduce or copy original photographs or drawings, and to all of them I want to express my sincere thanks; their names will be found in the figure captions and the notes on the plates.

In writing the book, I was aided greatly by a bibliography on underwater archaeology prepared for me by Mrs Helen Stabler. Those who have been kind enough to give advice, make helpful suggestions, or provide references include Alan B. Albright, E. Wyllys Andrews, Edwin C. Bearss, Stephan F. de Borhegyi, André Bouscaras, G. Roger Edwards, Mrs Anne Ellis, Anders Franzén, John Huston, Robert B. Inverarity, Gerhard Kapitän, Mustafa Kapkin, Edwin and Marion Link, Philip K. Lundeberg, David I. Owen, Ole Crumlin-Pedersen, Mendel Peterson, Mrs Brunilde Sismondo Ridgway, Linton Satterthwaite, Robert Scranton, Philippe Tailliez, Peter Throckmorton, Robert Wauchope, Lloyd P. Wells, and Robert C. Wheeler. To all of these, and certainly to others, I owe a great debt, but, because few of them will have seen previously what I have written, none should be held responsible for any parts of the book.

I wish also to thank those who enabled me to qualify for writing such a book as this. Dr Froelich Rainey, Director of the University Museum, and Dr Rodney S. Young, Chairman of the Department of Classical Archaeology at the University of Pennsylvania, first encouraged me to learn to dive, and have given their support ever since. My debt to Peter Throckmorton, who first showed me the marvels of underwater archaeology, can never be repaid. Sponsors with the foresight to support the Gelidonya and Yassi Ada excavations, when many considered underwater archaeology something less than scientific, include the American Philosophical Society, Mr William van Alen, the Catherwood Foundation, the Corning Museum of Glass, the Council of Underwater Archaeology, the Ford Foundation, Mr Nixon Griffis, the Haas Community Funds, the Lucius B. Littauer Foundation, Mr and Mrs James P. Magill, the National Geographic Society, the National Science Foundation, the Old Dominion Foundation, the Philadelphia Geographical Society, the Rockefeller Foundation, the Sarah Mellon Scaife Foundation, Mrs J. Lester Parsons, the Triopian Foundation, and the U.S. Navy. Only through the generous permission and assistance of the Turkish Department of Antiquities could this support have been used with the results to be described in the book.

A special word of mention should be made of the National Geographic Society, which has supported major pioneering efforts in underseas work from Beebe's bathysphere, through the aqualung research of Captain Cousteau and the photographic and sonic work of Harold Edgerton, to the present deep-diving experiments of Cousteau and Edwin Link. Further, they have supported underwater archaeological projects from the Canadian border to Mexico and Guatemala, and from the Pacific to the Mediterranean. The encouragement given by Dr Melvin M. Payne, President of the Society, has been most valuable to me, both in my own research and in writing this book.

Most of all my thanks must go to the ingenious and selfless members of the staff of the University Museum's excavation at Yassi Ada, whose loyalty to the pursuit of scientific underwater techniques and interpretation has produced so much of value, and to my wife Ann, whose tireless assistance both in America and Turkey has been truly remarkable.

G.F.B.

1. INTRODUCTION

At recent conferences on underwater archaeology suggestions have been made for a more attractive title to give this growing new field of research. None is completely suitable. 'Marine' or 'submarine' archaeology would limit the work to that done in the seas, while much has been done in rivers, lakes, and wells; 'hydroarchaeology' could include the study of ancient sources of water; and the hybrid 'aquaeology' is no closer to being an adequate title.

Archaeology under water, of course, should be called simply *archaeology*. We do not speak of those working on the top of Nimrud Dagh in Turkey as mountain archaeologists, nor those at Tikal in Guatemala as jungle archaeologists. They are all people who are trying to answer questions regarding man's past, and they are adaptable in being able to excavate and interpret ancient buildings, tombs, and even entire cities with the artifacts which they contain. Is the study of an ancient ship and its cargo, or the survey of toppled harbour walls somehow different? That such remains may lie under water entails the use of different tools and techniques in their study, just as the survey of a large area on land, using aerial photographs, magnetic detectors, and drills, requires a procedure other than excavating the stone artifacts and bones in a Palaeolithic cave. The basic aim in all these cases is the same. It is all archaeology.

Corinth was a famous Greek city whose life archaeologists have been recreating by uncovering and recording its architectural remains, by cataloguing and publishing its pottery and sculpture and coins, and by interpreting its inscriptions. Port Royal was a lively city in Jamaica which suddenly disappeared beneath the waves during a violent earthquake on 7 June 1692. In the study of its remains, walls and streets have been mapped, and objects of pottery, metal, and glass have been brought to the surface to be restored and preserved. Is there any difference between the two excavations except that in one case the excavator had to carry a supply of air strapped to his back?

Archaeologists often specialize in certain geographical, cultural or chronological areas, or they specialize in some aspect of antiquity such as architecture, writing, sculpture, or pottery, but no archaeologist specializes in the environment in which he works. Excavation in the arid regions of the American Southwest, for example, is no training for excavation in similar regions of the Near East. Yet the excavator who has worked under water, I have found, is often asked to work on sites merely because they lie under water. An inundated California Indian mound and a sunken ironclad gunboat of the nineteenth century have nothing in common, nor do the raising of an American dug-out canoe and the recovery of Ceylonese temple remains which have fallen into the sea. That certain diving or raising techniques are shared by all is no more important than that the same type of crane may be used to replace fallen temple blocks in Mexico and Greece; the crane operator does not then become an archaeologist specializing in architecture.

Just as certain techniques of digging stratigraphically, drawing plans, mending pottery, and dating by radiocarbon may be applicable to land sites throughout the world, so many of the techniques of working under water are also universal in their application. The techniques in both cases deserve to be published so that they may be used by others. A physicist may then specialize in radiocarbon dating, so that he may offer his technical services to any site, and in the same way a professional diver may offer his services to archaeology, but in neither case is the specialist usually the one to interpret the historical significance of the results. The specialist offers only information and advice to the archaeologist.

A defence of underwater archaeology as archaeology might seem unnecessary, but by some it has been considered something special, something just outside the field of true archaeology. Unfortunately a great deal of nonsense has been written about it. One distinguished archaeologist recently said that underwater archaeology is all rather silly, a view which he does not hold alone. Such a man might take great pains to excavate properly the drainage system of an ancient public building, studying the joins and diameters of the pipes in detail. Is the study of ancient ship construction less serious? The importance of ships to any maritime people is obvious, yet ships are often completely ignored in archaeology handbooks which cover subjects ranging from roof tiles to clothing, from fortification walls to jewellery, and from coins to furniture.

Knowledge to be gained from the water is not mainly of ship construction and trade routes, however, contrary to what has been written by even some most familiar with underwater excavations. Ignored by them is the unique knowledge of technology, art, and history which has come already from ancient cargoes. Virtually everything made by man, from tiny obsidian blades to huge temple columns, was carried at one time or another in a ship, and much was lost at sea. Other objects fell accidentally into lakes, wells, rivers, and seas, from cliffs, boats, and bridges, or were placed purposefully in the water as offerings to certain deities or for safe-keeping. Here also should be mentioned the remains on land which subsided, sometimes during earthquakes. But an archaeological site or artifact does not have to sink to be under water. Many are covered by rising water levels, especially in areas that have been inundated by man-made lakes.

Until fairly recently most of these sites and artifacts were considered suitable only for salvage. The term 'underwater archaeology' stirred up in the imagination the scene of adventurous and hardy men with great athletic ability but little else. The picture of sunken treasures being looted by amateur spear-fishermen came to mind. Such things did and do exist, but they are becoming less common. They follow the pattern of land excavation where early field archaeologists, also adventurous and hardy men, were often little more than hunters of antiquities; education and national antiquities' laws are beginning to preserve sites under water as they have done on land. The archaeologist today can blame no one but himself if underwater sites are left to amateurs. He has learned to drive a jeep, which can be as difficult and potentially dangerous as diving. The aqualung, invented over twenty years ago, only offers him a new method of getting to his site. He should remember, however, that it was the amateur, the diver, and not the professional archaeologist who led the way, found the sites, pioneered their excavation, and showed the promise of the future. We owe these amateur archaeologists a debt of gratitude in spite of errors they may have made.

There are noted divers, on the other hand, who still write that archaeologists cannot expect to dive well enough to excavate properly under water. I hope that this notion was dispelled forever by the work at Yassi Ada in Turkey, where an expedition recently completed nearly six thousand working dives on wrecks lying between 100 and 150 feet deep. For the first time a ship was excavated completely on the sea-bed, and it was done to the same exacting standards as are found on land. The expedition was staffed with people who normally would be found on any archaeological dig: archaeologists and archaeology students, several with land excavation experience, a classicist, an art historian, architects, draftsmen, and photographers. Many had never dived before arriving at the site. In addition there were a geologist, a medical doctor, and a mechanic, although through one three-month season the necessary machinery was well operated and maintained by archaeology students alone.

Ironically, the most advanced methods of making plans under water, so essential for any scientific excavation, were devised not by professional divers with years of experience in the sea, but by those who had just learned to dive for research. Often the advances were made only against the advice of the professionals who claimed that proposed methods were impossible. It is unfortunate that those who are simply divers, hoping to preserve their monopoly on underwater work, too often stress the difficulties in working under water. It takes years of training to become an archaeologist or an architect, however, and we train divers at Yassi Ada in little more than a week; naturally the new divers must work for a season under close supervision by an experienced staff member, for one cannot deny that there are hazards in diving. The safety measures taken by the staff are now much stricter than during the years when the diving was led by professional divers.

It is unwise to generalize, of course, but from more than fifty past staff members I have noticed that the best excavators were not necessarily the best divers. With one exception, on the other hand, none of those members who joined the staff primarily as divers had sufficient interest in scientific archaeology to continue for long their necessary but often dull tasks.

It is probably the development of mapping and excavating techniques mentioned above which has led to the charge that underwater archaeologists are overly concerned with gimmicks and gadgets, that technique is more important than historical results. Any archaeologist who has excavated both on land and under water, however, will realize the unique problems that must be overcome under water in order to obtain historical results. It is mainly the attempt to solve these problems which draws underwater excavators together in conferences on 'underwater archaeology'.

Another oft-quoted myth is that underwater archaeology is enormously expensive, costing, according to some authorities, up to ten times as much as work done on land. The excavation of the Bronze Age shipwreck at Cape Gelidonya, with its important results, however, cost no more than is spent annually on many land digs. The complete excavation of the Byzantine shipwreck at Yassi Ada, over a period of four summers, cost no more than is spent each year on several land excavations which come to mind. In both cases, much of the expense was on experimentation and on permanent equipment which can be used for later projects.

Thus we have seen that underwater archaeology offers a variety of ancient material comparable to that found on land, it should be conducted by ordinary archaeologists, and it often costs no more than land archaeology. The underwater archaeologist may be distinguished from his land-based colleague, therefore, only by the specialized techniques of excavation and preservation that are necessitated by the environment of the site on which he works. 'The problems presented by underwater archaeology,' wrote Dr Stephan de Borhegyi, whose work is described later, 'should be considered only as an extension of those already met and solved for dry-land archaeology.'

A book on archaeology under water must, therefore, be concerned primarily with techniques, just as are those books on aerial surveying for archaeology, physics for archaeology, and conservation for archaeology. This book is not, however, a technical manual. The time has not yet come when methods have been perfected to the extent that they may be presented as final solutions to the peculiar problems offered by each type of site. The book is written rather as a long essay on underwater archaeology to show what it is and how and why it has reached its present stage of development.

The book is divided into chapters which describe broad areas of techniques as used on actual projects. Within the chapters, there is no distinction between types of sites, such as sunken cities, shipwrecks or harbours, except as they define technical problems and solutions; a book on underwater archaeology cannot be, for example, a history of ship construction or of trade routes, either of which would have to include much evidence from sources not found beneath water.

Deciding what sites could be included in the book presented a problem. If a diver excavates 90 feet below the surface of the Mediterranean that is underwater archaeology. But if he stands only waist deep in a French harbour or a Danish fjord, is it still underwater archaeology? Or if he merely reaches with his hands into a spring or shallow stream and brings out well-preserved antiquities? Trying to decide at what depth underwater archaeology begins is the same as trying to decide how many whiskers make a beard, so I have decided to include here sites and artifacts that lie under any depth of water; almost all offer certain differences, if only in their state of preservation, from those found on dry land. I have also decided to include sites that lie under water during only part of the time in which they are studied; a ship which is raised intact to the surface, for example, may be examined exactly as if it were a land site, but underwater work was first necessary for its discovery and salvage.

Having decided what *could* be included in the book led to the question of what *should* be included, for it is not possible to describe every archaeological project which has taken place under water. Besides showing what archaeology under water is, I hope also to indicate its importance by presenting those sites that have yielded artifacts and information not likely to be found on land. At the same time, in order to give some idea of the wide range of underwater archaeology, I have tried to use, as examples of past work, sites from as many countries and periods as possible. This has caused the omission of many Mediterranean sites, which are the most numerous, but which are described most frequently in other publications. Therefore, I have had to stray far from my own speciality of Classical archaeology, and have quoted authorities more knowledgeable than I about the value of finds in other areas.

The reader already familiar with underwater archaeology may feel that the book is too tolerant in describing some past projects, for certainly all were not conducted scientifically. In such a new field of research, however, even the most serious archaeologists were bound to make many mistakes, and this is not the place to criticize their pioneering efforts. My hope is that the significant contributions of archaeology under water and the bright promise of its future will become evident from these pages.

2. WORKING IN THE UNDERWATER ENVIRONMENT

THE archaeologist has adapted himself to every kind of environment offered on our planet's surface, but none is so alien as that which he meets beneath the surface of its waters. The density of the water makes even a mild current more devastating than most winds he faces in open air; in a racing stream the diver must hold to firm objects to avoid being swept away completely. A muddy river offers a darkness that can be pierced by no flashlight. And, worst of all, the diver, if he is to breathe, must carry his own supply of air.

Yet it is largely because of this hostile environment that underwater archaeology is of such value. Artifacts which lie beneath the action of waves have been protected against certainly the most destructive of all agents – man, himself. Pottery cannot be broken through use when under water. Lead plating has not been torn from hulls of ancient ships, as lead clamps were broken from so many stone walls of the past. Far from the melting pots into which went so many masterpieces of ancient art, objects of copper and bronze and gold are well preserved. Marble has escaped the lime kilns. Wood and cloth are preserved in fresh water as they seldom are outside of desert sands or frozen northlands, and both are preserved even in our salty seas if they are covered quickly with mud or sand.

Some of the hardships of working under water can be compared to those faced above water. The underwater archaeologist protects himself against cold with a rubber suit rather than a coat. The infections he suffers from cuts and bruises are serious, but no more so than those he has contracted in steaming jungles. Divers searching for ancient sites have been frightened out of the water by sharks, but more than one surveyor on foot has been chased by wild boars and savage sheep dogs. The diver-excavator must beware of moray eels which live in empty wine jars, but no land-based excavator would in certain areas put his hand under a rock or piece of pottery without first checking for the scorpion which might linger there. Poisonous fish are to be avoided, as are equally dangerous snakes on land, and annoying worms that sting are the horse-flies of the underwater world.

Being surrounded by a liquid, with all that this implies, is the one hardship faced under water that cannot be compared to anything experienced on a land excavation. The diver cannot breathe unless he receives air from a tank on his back or from a hose running to the surface. Equally important is the weight, or pressure, of the water, which increases as the diver swims deeper. This pressure does not harm his body, which is mostly fluid and, therefore, no more compressible than the surrounding water, but it immediately begins to squeeze the air-filled spaces in his body, such as lungs, sinuses, and ear cavities. Under even a few feet of water he would not have the strength to expand his lungs and inhale air, even if it were present, unless it were at a pressure approximately the same as, or greater than, that of the water around him. Not many feet farther down his sinuses and ear cavities would be crushed.

The purpose of diving equipment of any kind is to provide air to the diver at a pressure which enables him to breathe, and which fills the cavities in his body with air equal in pressure to the water. The standard diver wears a metal helmet with a glass window or face-plate, screwed down to a rubberized canvas suit covering all but his hands. [Pl. 1] Air enters the helmet from a hose running to a compressor in a boat above and fills not only the helmet, but the entire suit above the waist. Naturally the diver becomes buoyant and would float to the surface like a bubble if he did not wear heavy lead weights on his chest, back, and shoes. Even so, he can float to the surface and pop out of the water if he does not operate properly the valve serving to bleed excess air out of the helmet through a non-return valve which keeps out water.

Helmeted sponge-divers have discovered most of the important underwater sites in the Mediterranean [Pl. 2], but their use in actual excavation is limited. In their bulky suits they lack the mobility so necessary for delicate work in fragmentary ships' hulls, and their leaden feet pose a constant threat to fragile objects. Their very weight, however, provides them with a firm base for

Figure 1. Scuba diver with air tanks, wet suit, knife, weight belt, depth gauge, wrist watch, mask, regulator, fins, clipboard, and graphite pencil. In box near grid are calipers, hammer, metre sticks, level, and object labels

heavy work, such as swinging a sledge-hammer onto a chisel to break away heavy sea-bed concretions.

Much simpler, much cheaper, and offering much greater freedom of movement than the gear just described is self-contained underwater breathing apparatus, known as scuba. [Fig. 1]. A number of types are available, but that most commonly used is the aqualung, developed by Emile Gagnan and Jacques-Yves Cousteau in 1942. The diver carries one or more metal tanks containing compressed air at a pressure of about a ton per square inch. The air comes out of the tank through a small hole and passes through a pressure-regulator to a hose which carries it to the diver's mouthpiece; exhalations containing dangerous carbon dioxide are exhausted immediately from the system. The regulator holds a rubber diaphragm which, under the increasing pressure of the water as the diver descends, allows more and more air to go to the diver. It is obvious that the deeper the diver goes, the more quickly will his air supply run out; all tanks, however, hold a reserve supply of air which can be obtained only by opening a special valve on the tank.

The scuba diver does not walk along the sea-bed as does the helmeted diver, but swims easily and quickly with flexible rubber fins worn on his feet. He maintains a proper balance in the water, so that he neither sinks nor rises, by means of a belt onto which he may attach as many lead weights as he needs. Covering his eyes and nose is a rubber mask with a glass face-plate; this allows him to see as clearly in clean water as he can see on land, except that everything is enlarged by one third because of the difference between the index of refraction of water and the index of refraction of air. It is important that the mask should fit over the nose so that the diver can exhale into it when necessary, equalizing the pressure of the surrounding water and avoiding the serious consequences of having the glass plate crushed against his face. For the same reason he should never wear the ear-plugs some swimmers use for, under water, these would be pushed into his ears.

For protection against cold the scuba diver generally wears a neoprene rubber suit, consisting of pants and jacket, with long or short sleeves, as well as boots and hood. This is known as a 'wet suit', because it does not keep the diver dry. Although it should fit snugly, the wet suit allows a thin layer of water to creep in next to the diver's skin. The water, quickly warmed by the diver's body, then acts as an excellent insulator. Another kind of suit, the 'dry suit', fits so snugly around the wrists, ankles, and face that it keeps all water out; long underwear may be worn under it, and it is superior to the wet suit for dives in extremely cold water. Even in the relatively warm Mediterranean, a suit is usually needed because of the rapidity with which water absorbs heat from the human body.

On his wrists the diver wears a waterproof watch, a depth

gauge, and, if he is searching for a site or swimming away from a known point, a compass. A strong knife should be worn on the leg or at the waist to cut away possibly entangling lines or seaweed. Other equipment, such as a long club to fend off sharks or an underwater flashlight, are carried if called for.

There are other types of scuba. One, the oxygen-rebreather, is used by Navy divers in wartime to avoid releasing tell-tale bubbles. Exhaled air is breathed back through a tube and through a chemical filter which removes the carbon dioxide. At the same time, pressurized oxygen is added to the air as it is again breathed by the diver, to replace the oxygen which his body has burned up in activity. This type of equipment is extremely dangerous for the uninitiated, and it should not be used below 25 feet because of the often fatal oxygen poisoning which comes from breathing oxygen under pressure.

A compromise between standard diving equipment and scuba is known as a *hookah* or *narghile*, named after the Turkish water pipe for obvious reasons [Pl. 4]. It is exactly the same as scuba, except that air is supplied to the regulator not by tanks but from a hose running to a compressor on the surface. This provides an excellent method of diving on sites where the diver does not have to move far from one spot, for there is no danger of his running out of air, there is constant communication with the hose tender on the boat or barge above by means of signals pulled on a line, there is less danger of explosion from pressure, and the compressors needed to pump air to a diver are cheaper and more reliable than those needed to fill high-pressure tanks.

So far we have discussed only the problem of pressure as it applies to the diver's ability to breathe, but there are other equally important problems. As the diver descends and breathes increasingly more highly pressurized air, he is breathing more of the nitrogen which comprises about 80 per cent of the air. This nitrogen causes a definite dulling of the brain, known as nitrogen narcosis, which has many of the same symptoms as are caused by drinking alcohol; every additional 50 feet of depth, according to one rule, is equal to one more dry martini. Susceptibility varies among people, but most notice the effects at 100 feet, and diving to 200 feet or deeper poses a real threat even to experienced divers. Divers have been known to remove their mouthpieces for no apparent reason at great depths. The narcosis disappears as the diver ascends, if he has the presence of mind to do so.

Although narcosis can cause errors in measurements and impair judgement at 120 feet, I have not known it to affect excavation at that depth among divers who knew their jobs well enough to do them almost by routine. While mapping a wreck in 150 feet of water, for example, a man must rehearse in his mind exactly what he plans to do during each fifteen-minute dive, as if he were memorizing a scene from a play. Once on the bottom it is frustrating to see a partner who has not planned his moves in advance, but who has only a general idea of what is to be done, swimming to the wrong end of the wreck, driving stakes into the wrong places, and completely wasting that dive.

Although the effects of narcosis decrease as the diver swims upward, at the end of each dive, it is then that he faces the great danger of suffering decompression sickness, commonly known as 'the bends'. The air he has been breathing has been absorbed naturally by his blood while his body was under pressure. This in itself does not cause a problem as long as the diver remains at depth, but he must not rise quickly to the surface. One need only pull the cork from a champagne bottle to see why : the pressure is released suddenly, allowing the gas in the champagne to come out of solution and form bubbles. In the same way, bubbles can form in the blood of the rapidly ascending diver, possibly to kill or paralyse him.

'The bends' may be avoided only by ascending according to schedules published by various navies of the world. These give the diver a chance to breathe off gradually the pressurized air in his system. The deeper the diver goes, or the longer he stays down, the more air he absorbs and, therefore, the more slowly he must come up. According to the U.S. Navy Standard Air Decompression Table, if a diver dives to 100 feet for 40 minutes (timed from the moment he starts down from the surface), he must at the end of his dive take one and a half minutes to arrive at a point just 10 feet below the surface, and there he must remain for 15 minutes before going on to the surface. If he dives to the same depth for 50 minutes, however, he must swim up to a point 20 feet below the surface in one and a third minutes, and there remain for 2 minutes; then he goes on up to a 10-foot depth and stays for 24 minutes before he can leave the water. But if a diver goes down to 180 feet for the same 50 minutes, he must make decompression stops of varying lengths of time every 10 feet below the surface, starting at a depth of 50 feet; the total decompression time for the 50-minute dive is over two hours.

Use of diving schedules, printed as tables, does not eliminate all possibility of 'the bends', but it greatly reduces it. Since Laurence Joline, probably the most safety-conscious of my staff at Yassi Ada, was paralysed temporarily from the waist down, even while using the tables with a safety margin, I have followed a number of suggestions made to me by a noted diving physiologist. An examination of each staff member is made by the expedition doctor, who has the final word at any time on whether or not any person may dive; the divers are encouraged to get a good night's sleep by having the camp electric generator turned off at a certain hour each night; there is one day of rest a week on which no diving is allowed; except for the night before the day of rest, no beer, wine or strong alcohol is allowed; and the standard Navy tables are used with a great safety margin. If a dive is to 100 feet, for example, we read the tables for the next greater depth, or 110 feet; if a dive is for 30 minutes, we go to the next longer time on the tables, or 40 minutes. Thus we often decompress for twice as long as might be thought necessary, but after thousands of dives without incident while using this system, my staff would be reluctant to change.

The only cure for 'the bends' is to be placed under pressure again, and to have the pressure reduced very gradually, following special recompression schedules. Every diving operation should have a recompression chamber for this treatment, and every diver should know how to use the chamber [Pl. 3]. Dives should never take place unless there are enough people on the diving boat or barge, excluding the medical doctor who must be free to make examinations and decisions, to open the chamber, place a stricken diver inside, seal the door, and begin to fill it with compressed air in a short period of time. Weekly 'chamber drills' are highly recommended, although it is probably not wise to subject the 'patient' to actual pressure when it is not necessary. At Yassi Ada, we never dive without a spare compressor to insure continuous air in case of engine failure to the first, and an emergency supply of filled high-pressure air tanks is kept on hand.

The chamber also serves to treat another dreaded diving disorder, air embolism. If a diver rises to the surface while holding his breath for any reason, perhaps through panic, the air inside him will expand as the pressure around him decreases, thus rupturing his lungs. Death occurs almost at once in many cases, and may be caused by an improper ascent from less than 10 feet of water. Embolisms are best avoided by the training which instills confidence in the divers, and by thorough medical examination to insure their lungs are not diseased.

Other diving disorders can be found in any diver's handbook, but an understanding of those mentioned is essential for an appreciation of the concern for improved excavating techniques. One may imagine the frustration that would be felt by any archaeologist who could visit his site on land for only about 45 minutes a day, in two trips! Yet that is the length of time it is economical to dive on a site in 120 feet of water. Certainly more efficient methods of mapping and surveying than those used on land are needed under water, and new tools, such as the air lift or 'underwater vacuum cleaner', must take the place of shovels and wheelbarrows.

The limited amount of time that each excavator can spend on a site, at the depths where shipwrecks are most often found in the sea, also necessitates a larger staff of trained archaeologists than is normally found on land excavations of comparable size. On land one supervisor may have from two or three to twenty or thirty workmen under his control. He guides the work and takes notes as the excavation progresses. Under water, however, the archaeologist can remain no longer than any one shift of divers, and it has proved often unwise to leave decisions to those untrained in archaeology. For that reason, at least one of each team of divers should be sufficiently knowledgeable to make decisions without the advice of the director, who can himself visit the site only twice a day.

Because the archaeologist in charge of any aspect of an excavation cannot see what has been accomplished on each dive, and because if he has even a minor cold he may be unable to dive for days at a time, daily developing and printing of underwater photographs is essential for centralized control of the work. Almost any good camera may be used as long as it is encased in a water-tight housing, a wide variety of which are commercially available; there is also at least one camera, requiring no special encasement, which may be used either on land or under water. In each type of underwater camera it should be remembered that the side of the lens facing the film is dry, while the other side of the lens faces water. The difference between the indices of refraction of water and of air, demonstrated by the apparent 'bending' of a stick in a glass of water, causes some distortion which may be corrected by specially ground lenses if desired.

Water absorbs light rays more quickly than air, and removes certain colours before others. Under only a few feet of water red fades away, and then orange and later yellow disappear so that the diver and camera see everything in various hues of blue. If colour is desired in photographs, it may be obtained by artificial lighting from either flood lights or flash bulbs. The photographer should not place the source of light next to his camera, however, for the light might then reflect directly onto the camera lens from minute and otherwise unnoticeable particles in the water. To avoid the resultant effect of 'snow', an assistant should hold the camera flash unit, attached to the camera by means of a long wire, to one side of the object or area to be photographed.

The underwater archaeologist may also keep a constant watch on his excavation by closed-circuit television, or by travelling to his site by methods other than diving. He may, for example, descend in a chamber or small submarine. The chamber allows the archaeologist to remain all day on the sea-bed if he wishes, observing the work through thick glass or plastic ports, and directing each team of divers by means of an underwater communications system; this would be particularly useful on extremely deep salvage operations where only the most highly skilled divers should work with their special breathing equipment. The chamber is enclosed so that its occupant remains at atmospheric pressure and does not have to decompress or risk suffering 'the bends' at the end of his long stays on the bottom. The small submarine offers the same advantages as the chamber, but has the additional asset of being able to move freely without ties to the surface. In all these cases the archaeologist should also dive, if at all possible, in order to follow the work more closely. His greatest control, however, will come from the selection of a trusted archaeological staff.

Undoubtedly the major difference between excavating under water and on land is the constant emotional and mental strain of the former. No matter what duties the director may delegate to others, the ultimate responsibility for the maintenance and safe operation of boats, barges, compressors, winches, chambers, generators, diving gear, and countless other pieces of equipment is his, and he knows that lives as well as accurate records may depend on his decisions. Divers died at Antikythera, Artemision, and Grand Congloué, and divers suffered serious cases of 'the bends', luckily cured, at Yassi Ada, Dzibilchaltun, Kyrenia, and Albenga, all sites to be discussed later; death has certainly been avoided at other sites only by alert diving partners. Diving is a very serious and complex business and offers little opportunity for relaxation.

Why then does the diving archaeologist risk such hazards as have been described? It is not for adventure. If the same material, in the same quantity, in the same state of preservation, and in the same excellently dated contexts were to be found on land, most archaeologists would surely prefer to excavate it there. But it is not found on land.

ARCHAEOLOGICAL surveys of various kinds are made on land. Archaeologists, singly or in small groups, cover hundreds of square miles by jeep, bicycle, mule, canoe and foot while locating and mapping all the visible sites in certain areas; samplings of surface artifacts reveal the nature of habitation sites. More complex teams use core samplers and analyse the pollen in large areas to determine if the regions were forested, cultivated, or barren during the different periods of antiquity. The general aim is the same : to study the pattern of habitation for various periods and cultures, and to select promising sites for more thorough study by excavation. Clues may be provided by tracing ancient sources of water, or by investigating natural harbours or naturally fortified high points. Aerial survey can play a large part in such work by spotting sites otherwise inaccessible because of jungle, or invisible except by the crop and soil marks which can be seen from the air.

Some archaeologists survey for particular types of sites, such as prehistoric rock shelters, Classical fortresses, coastal trading posts, or burial mounds, although non-pertinent but interesting discoveries are also recorded by such specialized surveyors. An example of such investigations is that of the Italian industrialist, Carlo Lerici, who has developed a means of boring a hole into the ground wherever it seems likely that there is an Etruscan tomb below. A periscope is then slipped into the hole for a first look and, if warranted, a tiny camera is lowered into the tomb to photograph it completely.

Still other archaeologists are looking for specific sites which may be known from historical records and identified by their geographic positions, as was the case with Gordion in Turkey. In such instances, specialized equipment can be of value. The joint team of the Lerici Foundation of Milan and the University of Pennsylvania Museum tested ultrasonic devices, magnetic

gradiometers, electrical resistivity meters, and the proton magnetometer in locating buried walls during its successful search for
the lost city of Sybaris in southern Italy.

Locally obtained information and rumour play a large part in
all types of surveys. In his search for the capital of the Inca
Empire, Hiram Bingham paid Peruvian guides fifty cents a day
to lead him to the ruins which they knew. The result was the
magnificent discovery of Machu Picchu, high in the Andes. Even
illiterate farmers often have a great fund of information about
artifacts and tombs they have uncovered while digging wells or
ploughing.

All of the types of surveys described above can be, and have
been, made under water. General surveys of selected coastal areas
and inland lakes and rivers have plotted the distribution of
Roman anchors in Mediterranean harbours, located Spanish galleons in the Gulf of Mexico and the Caribbean, and turned up
countless artifacts of early American Indians and settlers. The
lack of organization among the amateur divers who have found
most of these remains is understandable in such a new discipline,
and already corrective steps are being taken. A permanent committee, with representative archaeologists from Spain, Italy, and
France, has been established to keep a map of sites found in
the Western Mediterranean, and a standard form for the reporting of new finds has been suggested for amateur surveyors. In
America, the Council of Underwater Archaeology in San
Francisco collected information on promising sites until the recent
death of John Huston, its founder; hopefully it will soon be
revived.

In spite of these efforts, there will always be the unwelcome
treasure and souvenir hunters, as on land. Education of amateurs
through their diving clubs must be regarded as a responsibility of
local archaeologists if general surveys are to prove meaningful.
What may be accomplished by serious amateurs is shown by the
Archaeological Section of the British Sub-Aqua Club, which tells
its members that all artifacts found in the River Thames must be
plotted on a 50-inch Ordnance Survey chart and then turned over
to a museum. Already they have brought from the muddy bottom
objects dating from prehistoric to medieval and later periods

Figure 2. Underwater sites in Europe and the Mediterranean

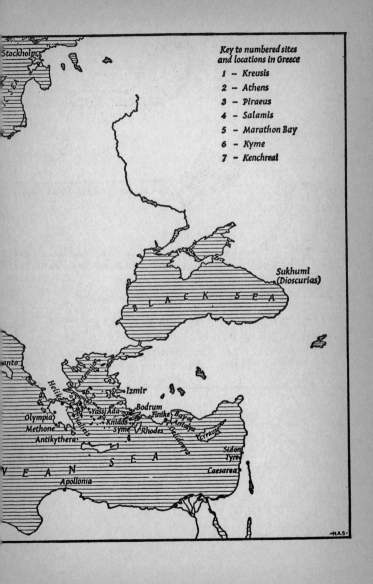

Key to numbered sites
and locations in Greece

1 – Kreusis
2 – Athens
3 – Piraeus
4 – Salamis
5 – Marathon Bay
6 – Kyme
7 – Kenchreai

Stockholm

Sukhumi
(Dioscurias)

BLACK   SEA

anto

Izmir

Helike

Olympia   Yassi Ada   Bodrum   Finike   Bay of
Methone   Knidos   Antalya
                 Syme   Rhodes   CYPRUS
Antikythera

Sidon
Tyre
Caesarea

EAN   SEA

Apollonia

–H.A.S–

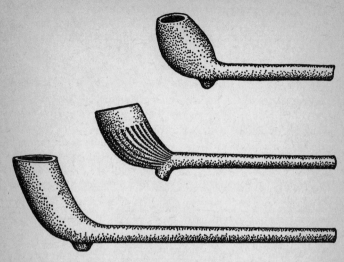

Figure 3. Pipes from the River Thames (after Forrest-Webb)

[Fig. 3]. But whether or not such finds will result in archaeological conclusions not to be reached more easily by land surveys,
it is too early to know. The following examples are of specific
surveys which could have been made only under water.

Nearly a third of the fresh-water lakes in the United States
have been artificially created, and dam-building projects will soon
double that amount. Salvage operations can save only a fraction
of the sites which will be flooded; when the Committee for the
Recovery of Archaeological Remains was established in 1945,
over one hundred new dams were planned just for the Missouri
River and its tributaries.

Donald P. Jewell is particularly interested in the sites in the
foothills of California which are fast disappearing as the exploding
population in that state demands more and more fresh water.
The area had not been thoroughly excavated before being inundated and, because the Indians of California were so culturally
and so dialectically diversified, Jewell realized that 'the inundation
of one large valley could eliminate the remnants of an entire
culture that had existed in California for thousands of years'.

He began to look under water. The submerged sites are sometimes visible from the air because of the dark 'clouds' of suspended material which hang over the refuse heaps, or middens, if they are in quiet water. Usually, however, Jewell has to locate his sites visually while diving. Attached by a line to a drum placed vertically on the lake bed, he swims in decreasing circles with his face just above the bottom until he has reached the drum. In situations where this has proved impracticable, especially where silting has occurred, he has resorted to bringing up tell-tale midden traces, such as bones, cooking stones, and stone implements, in the metal jaws of a Peterson grab dropped from a raft. Core samplers have proved less successful in his limited operation, but could be effective in some cases. Jewell realizes that better methods of surveying in these conditions may soon be developed, but he is working against time in his effort to prevent a gap in our knowledge of prehistoric California. Silting may make some of the mounds still less noticeable. Even worse, dredging operations to clear such silt could very well dredge away entire villages, while sites which lie in currents may be eroded completely. Until that happens, Jewell marks each promising area with a balloon float and triangulates its position from shore. The excavation which follows is primitive by land standards, but only through such experimentation will the means be found to gain further knowledge of areas soon to be submerged; the vast tract which the Nile waters behind the Aswan Dam will swallow up is a case in point.

New knowledge of American Indians in more northerly regions may be the indirect result of a completely different type of survey which has been active since 1960. From the late seventeenth century until the middle of the nineteenth century, large canoes laden with trade goods for the Indians were paddled westward from Montreal. At Grand Portage, on the northwest side of Lake Superior, the goods were packaged and sent still farther along the lakes and rivers between present Minnesota and Ontario. The hardy men who braved this three-thousand-mile waterway for the fur companies are known as voyageurs. Portages of their canoes and goods where waters were impassable could not have been pleasant; nearly two hundred pounds is no easy load, even with frequent rest stops. It must have been a great temptation to shoot the rapids rather than walk around them, but the toll was a heavy one. A diary of 1800 mentions that at almost every rapid passed during the twenty-five day trip from Montreal a cross had been erected, and that at one rapid there were as many as thirty crosses. Other journals of the same period recount actual instances of canoes turning over, and the quantities of goods that were lost. Although Dr E. W. Davis is neither a professional archaeologist nor a historian, he has had a long and keen interest in the history of the fur trade in Minnesota. In 1960 he watched three local scuba divers searching for a shipwreck in Lake Superior; before the day was out he had conceived the idea of searching for remains where the voyageurs might have suffered calamities, and had asked the young divers to help him in his plan. Selecting areas which seemed suitably dangerous, his new assistants began to dive along portions of the fur trade route, hanging onto rocks in the cold, fast waters to keep from being swept downstream. [Pl. 5] At Horsetail Rapids, in about 15 feet of water, one of the divers spotted an overturned kettle, but this proved to be only the outermost of nine brass and copper kettles nested neatly together. [Pls. 6, 7] Such nests of kettles are known from the lists of merchandise on licence applications for the fur trade. That the kettles were important to the traders is also known from the late-eighteenth-century journal of a fur trader who, after wintering alone with the Indians, wrote : 'The principal difficulty we laboured under was the want of a kettle.'

The discovery of the first nest of kettles gave the group high hopes of finding much more, and the story of all that followed shows a partnership between amateurs and professionals which should serve as a model for others. The kettles were given to the Minnesota Historical Society, which sent its assistant director, Robert C. Wheeler, to lead a search on a larger scale. The Royal Ontario Museum became a partner in a joint effort to search for trade items along the United States-Canada border, and soon other foundations and departments, including the National Geographic Society, became involved.

Forty miles from Horsetail Rapids are the Basswood Rapids, considered to be extremely dangerous by travellers of the late

Key to numbered sites
1 - Basswood Rapids
2 - Horsetail Rapids
3 - Granite River

Grand Portage
1 2 3

Montreal

L. Champlain

L. George

York R.

Yazoo R.

Vicksburg

St. Marks R.

0
500 miles
0
800 km.

H.A.S.

Figure 4. Underwater sites in North America

eighteenth century. There the same three divers who had found
the kettles came upon the contents of an overturned canoe, no
longer packaged, but close together on the rocky bottom: thirty-
five iron trading axes and twenty-four iron chisels and spears

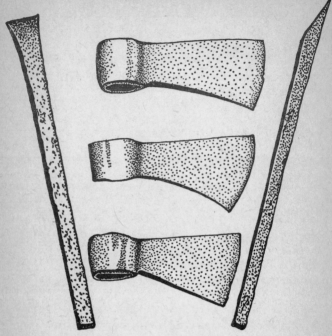

Figure 5. Iron trade axes and chisels from the Basswood River (after photos courtesy R. Wheeler)

[Fig. 5]. Near by, probably from the same canoe, were about a thousand lead musket balls, lead shot, buttons, thimbles, cloth fragments, knives, beads, whetstones, gunflints, facial pigments, and more. The rushing waters in which these objects were found have not allowed the use of grids or conventional excavating techniques; it seems, however, that the objects collect among the rocks wherever the water carries them, and so far no remains of canoes have been found. That such canoes were lost is no surprise, and many of the objects found were already known from contemporary lists of goods. Is their raising, then, anything more than antiquities-collecting?

The archaeological value of such a survey is great, for the well-preserved artifacts often must represent the trade items from one overturned canoe. Alan Woolworth, curator of the Minnesota Historical Society's museum, has said that 'the evolutionary development of such everyday things as kettles, their places of origin, the manufacturing techniques used, as well as prices and distribution patterns, are only incompletely understood'. Now, if a musket or other known object from a canoe can be dated, then the other parts of the cargo, which should be roughly contemporary, can likewise be dated; it is also possible that documentary evidence for the dates of some of the disasters may be found among old records. Further, since such trade items more often than not did reach the Indians, similar items found in Indian sites will allow better dating of those sites, thereby providing a firmer chronological framework for many of the prehistoric remains of the American North.

Another fruitful collaboration between amateur divers and professional archaeologists began with the discovery by Manfred Töpke of a clay incense burner in Lake Amatitlan, Guatemala [Pl. 11]. Between 1955 and 1957, Töpke and his Guatemalan diving companions raised hundreds of well-preserved pieces of pottery and stone sculpture from the lake. Dr Stephan de Borhegyi, Director of the Milwaukee Public Museum, was then consulted. The ensuing survey brought to light, among other things, beautifully preserved incense burners decorated with designs of Maya gods and a wide variety of plant and animal life [Pls. 9, 10, Figs. 6, 7]. One vessel, containing liquid mercury, pieces of cinnabar and graphite, and smashed jade ear spools, seemed to be proof that some of the objects had been cast into the water as offerings to the lake gods. Another vessel contained part of a girl's skull, suggesting human sacrifice, at least in secondary form. Still other vessels, imbedded on the lake floor, seem to have been carried by flowing lava from the shore where they had been placed to placate the active volcano Pacaya which overlooks the lake.

In addition to throwing valuable light on Maya religious practices, the lake finds may assist in the dating of known types of pottery from land sites. Because the divers had accurately catalogued their original finds, it was possible to determine that these had come from nine separate deposits; seven of these deposits were near natural hot springs which today serve as thermal baths, but which once may have awed the inhabitants of the area. De Borhegyi noted that the finds from each of the deposits were typologically and, therefore, probably chronologically different. He further guessed that the deposits were contemporary with adjacent habitations on the land around the lake, and a survey of known and newly discovered sites proved this to be so; as the settlements were moved from place to place through the centuries, the offering places followed them. This suggested more strongly than ever that the offerings in each underwater deposit were contemporaneous, but problems arose. All the pottery from one site, for example, seemed to be Early Classic (A.D. 300–

Figure 6. Effigy censer from Lake Amatitlan; A.D. 600–900 (after de Borhegyi)

Figure 7. Effigy censer cover in shape of anthropomorphic jaguar god; from Lake Amatitlan (A.D. 400–600) (after de Borhegyi)

Figure 8. Underwater sites in Central America and the Caribbean

600) in date, yet among the pottery were seated stone figures of a type which, when found on land, were considered to be Late Classic (A.D. 600–900) and possibly not Maya in origin. Only further work, both on land and under water, will clarify such problems.

From Mexico's Lake Chapala have come miniature vessels of a type not usually found on land, indicating that they were made especially for ceremonial purposes, and clay statues have been recovered from Lake Guija on the border between Guatemala and El Salvador. That this practice of throwing ceremonial objects into lakes had an early beginning is suggested to de Borhegyi by an incense burner of Early Pre-Classical type found in Lake

Ixpaco in Guatemala. These are but hints of what may be found by future surveys of Middle American Lakes.

So far we have discussed general surveys and surveys for particular types of sites, but specific sites on land, such as Biblical and Classical cities, are often located with the aid of written records. Documentary evidence has led also to the discovery of a number of specific underwater sites. One such was the resting-place of the gunboat *Cairo*, whose finding will be described with her raising in the next chapter. Another was the site of the two oldest known wrecks in the Americas – from Columbus's last voyage to the New World.

In 1503 Columbus sailed the *Capitana* and *Santiago* aground in St Anne's Bay, Jamaica; these were the only ships remaining from the four with which he had left Spain the year before, and even they were in no shape to allow him to continue. For a year he awaited rescue, and when it finally came he abandoned the two ships to settle deeper and deeper into the mud. The wrecks lay covered and untouched until 1966, when Bob Marx and his wife struck a wooden timber while swimming over the bottom with metal probes. Marx had been diving for archaeology already in Jamaica, excavating the sunken city of Port Royal, and he was intimately familiar with Columbus's records; a few years earlier he had crossed the Atlantic in a replica of the *Nina*. Now, with samples of pottery and wood raised from a test pit, he called on other scientists for help. Professor Harold Edgerton, of the Massachusetts Institute of Technology, criss-crossed the area and defined the positions of the two ships with his famous mud-penetrating sonar. Dr John Sanders, of Columbia University's Hudson Laboratories, sent one of his corers and a diver to operate it; cores of Edgerton's targets brought up more wood and pottery, along with glass, bone, and ballast stones. Analyses and studies of these fragments all point to one conclusion : Marx has found two of Columbus's ships. Their planned excavation is eagerly awaited.

Still another underwater site found with the aid of documents is that of the seventeen-century warship *Vasa*, found by Anders Franzén in Stockholm Harbour. Franzén, a petroleum engineer for the Swedish Admiralty, guessed that the Baltic Sea might contain well-preserved ancient ships because its low salt content does not support teredos, the shipworms which quickly destroy wooden remains in most seas and oceans. After years of reading naval history, Franzén selected for search a dozen ships from the sixteenth and seventeenth centuries, the time when Sweden rose to be a world power. In 1953 he began his survey, motoring back and forth over Stockholm Harbour in an open boat, sometimes using wire sweeps and grapnels, and later using a small core sampler which he had invented to bring up plugs of wood if it hit old ships. The following year he discovered a report to King Gustav Adolphus II which described the sinking of the Vasa.

The king had ordered the Vasa to be constructed in 1625 by private shipbuilders in the Royal Naval Dockyard. The builders, who at that time worked only with general specifications rather than with plans, produced by 1627 a 180-foot square-rigger which displaced 14,000 tons and carried sixty-four cannon. The year after her launching, with ballast and armaments added, the Vasa began her maiden voyage with not only her crew, but many of their families who were allowed to attend the event. Within the first few hundred yards, however, she was hit by a sudden wind, heeled over, flooded, and sank. The captain and other commanding officers, along with the shipwrights, were arrested and brought to trial, but none were indicted by the Court of Enquiry.

The Vasa was included in the list of a dozen ships which Franzén had collected, and he began to concentrate on it. Two years later, in 1956, he caught a piece of black oak with his core sampler; it was so near the site of the reported disaster that Swedish Navy divers were sent down to investigate. The plug of wood did, indeed, come from the Vasa, which became the oldest known fully identified ship [Pl. 12].

The Vasa has since been raised to the surface, as described in Chapter IV, but Anders Franzén has been asked, as have almost all underwater explorers, why it was necessary to go under water. The Vasa was a comparatively recent ship. Would it not be far simpler to study the plans of contemporary ships, and even to rebuild one? Surprisingly, however, ship's drawings did not become common until the eighteenth century and, as Franzén has pointed out, 'the experts are not even agreed on the system of measurement used in shipbuilding' before that time. Even accurate paintings of contemporary ships are rare.

Howard Chapelle, Curator of the Division of Transportation in the United States National Museum, points out, moreover, that even after ships' plans began to be made, all too few were kept. There is little documentary evidence for ships and boats in America, for example, before 1800, and many types of small boats are not to be found at all in old plans. It is possible that only through underwater archaeology will we fill the gaps in our knowledge of such comparatively recent ships.

Of older ships we know much, much less. In his search for the remains of such ships, Peter Throckmorton turned to perhaps the most valuable source of information for archaeological surveyors: local inhabitants. For dry land archaeologists they are the farmers and shepherds; for the underwater archaeologist they are the fishermen, sponge divers, and sponge draggers.

Throckmorton, a New York photo-journalist, arrived in Turkey in 1958 with both diving and land excavation experience, as well as anthropology courses, behind him. He was drawn to Bodrum (ancient Halikarnassos), therefore, both because of his interest in the divers who made it the sponge centre of Turkey and because of a bronze bust, perhaps of the goddess Demeter, which a Bodrum sponge dragger had pulled from the sea in his net [Pl. 23]. The statue had been seen lying on a beach by the English archaeologist George Bean and had been placed in the Izmir Museum just five years before. Throckmorton joined forces with members of the Izmir Fishmen's Club, including Mustafa Kapkin and Rasim Divanli, who had abandoned earlier thoughts of searching for the wreck that had yielded the statue because of inadequate equipment. Several attempts that year to locate the captain who had made the find, however, were fruitless; he was always at sea.

But the luck at Bodrum was far from being all bad. Throckmorton and Kapkin made friends with Captain Kemal Aras, a sponge diver whose many years at sea had made him intimately familiar with the coast. Captain Kemal invited them to sail with him on his boat, *Mandalinçi*, and promised to show them the remains which he had seen during many years of walking the sea bottom in his search for sponges. These all lay within the range of helmeted divers and, therefore, of the explorers with their aqualungs; many of the sites known only from draggers' nets were far too deep. For a summer Throckmorton and Kapkin sailed on the *Mandalinçi*, diving often alone and without proper equipment, sharing the life of the sponge divers crowded into the 38-foot boat, and learning of the deaths from 'the bends' which take place only too often every year among the Bodrum divers. At the end of their trip they had recorded more than thirty wrecks or possible wrecks of ancient ships, mostly wine carriers, dating from Hellenistic to Medieval times.

The first area visited was probably the most promising. Yassi Ada (Flat Island) is a tiny, barren island about sixteen miles up the coast from Bodrum by boat. It would be unworthy of notice except for the treacherous reef which extends from it, in places only six feet below the waves. How many ships have ripped their bottoms open on the reef is difficult to know at present, but it is more than a dozen. On the top of the reef, Ottoman cannon balls are mixed with wine amphoras of about the time of Christ. Near the reef, at a depth of 120 feet, Throckmorton saw the cargo of a ship which had sailed during the lifetime of Mohammed, and a few feet away, in 140 feet of water, a cargo about three centuries older; because these two wrecks lay on a sandy bottom, Throckmorton rightly guessed that a good portion of their wooden hulls would be preserved beneath the sand, and that they would be especially suitable for future excavation. Several years later, a third wreck of the 16th century was found under only a few inches of sand between the two. Elsewhere, an estimated ton of coloured glass ingots, some larger than a man's head, had been raised by sponge divers. Some of these are now in the Bodrum Museum and other bits are to be found scattered over the reef, but most of the ingots were sold to an Izmir glass factory and the wreck which would allow their dating has yet to be found. It is no wonder that Throckmorton called the area a veritable graveyard of ancient ships.

The greatest find for Throckmorton was to come more slowly, and it was not by accident. In his log he noted Captain Kemal's description of a wreck near Finike, on the southwest coast. The wreck was particularly intriguing because of the mention of

Figure 9. The Towvane

bronze spearheads and pieces of bronze over a metre long which were so old they were unrecognizable. The mass of material was stuck together, but Captain Kemal considered dynamiting it for its scrap value. Everything about the wreck suggested great age, but Captain Kemal did not have plans for revisiting the area that year and Throckmorton had no means to visit it without him. He could only write in his log that this seemed to be the most important site to be examined.

The following summer, through Virginia Grace, the American amphora expert, and Stanton Waterman, the well-known underwater cine-photographer, Throckmorton was put in touch with a diving expedition headed by Drayton Cochran, and he was able to guide Cochran's boat to the spot near Finike. For two days the divers combed the area sketched out in advance by Captain Kemal.

Nothing was seen and the expedition planned to move on. Finally, on the last planned dive, Susan Phipps and Cochran's son John spotted the cargo heavily overgrown at a depth of 90 feet. Mustafa Kapkin dived and made a hasty plan which later proved to be surprisingly accurate. Samples brought to the surface and recorded were soon assigned to the Late Bronze Age. The complete excavation of the site, described in a later chapter, dated the cargo to about 1200 B.C. It was the oldest shipwreck ever found.

The search for the wreck which yielded the 'Demeter' bust did not stop. In 1965 I arrived in Turkey to direct an underwater survey for the University of Pennsylvania Museum and the National Geographic Society. With me were an underwater television system, a proton magnetometer, a Towvane, and a small group of technicians. We planned, at the same time, to look for another deep wreck which had just produced a bronze Negro youth [Pl. 24] and a statuette of the goddess Fortuna. On board our rented trawler, as guides, were the three sponge captains who had netted the three statues.

Daily we towed the television camera just above the bottom in each of the search areas, watching the sea bed move by on a monitor screen inside the trawler cabin. We also used the Towvane [Fig. 9], a one-man observation capsule, shaped something like the early Mercury space capsules except that it has movable vanes, or wings, protruding from its sides. The observer/pilot sat inside, breathing air supplied from tanks and scrubbed of carbon dioxide by a chemical absorbant, as he was pulled on the end of a 1,000-foot nylon line. By depressing or raising the forward edges of the vanes, with control wheels inside, the pilot could make the Towvane plane upward or downward through the water. He was warned, by telephone, of any large rocks or other obstructions spotted with a fathometer mounted on the trawler, which was naturally several hundred feet ahead.

In two months we saw only sand and seaweed, and the proton magnetometer revealed no metal remains. We were discouraged, but we had learned two important lessons. First, the sponge captains could only direct us to areas several square miles in size, far too large to be surveyed effectively with visual methods which allowed search paths no more than thirty feet wide. Secondly, we learned that the sea bed in each of the areas was almost perfectly flat, ideal for searching with side-scanning sonar.

In 1967 we returned with a team from the Scripps Institution of Oceanography. They towed a side-scanning sonar which bounced sound waves off the sea bed out to 600 feet on either side of the trawler. Now our search paths were 1,200 feet wide rather than 30, and the 'Demeter' area was covered in only a week. Over a dozen protrusions on the sea bed were recorded on a paper graph of the sound waves, but we couldn't know if these were wrecks or only rock outcroppings. Only two days were spent in the area where the Negro boy and Fortuna had been found, and there one excellent target was recorded about a mile off shore.

During the search three shore-based transit operators, about a mile apart, had followed the trawler with their sights and radioed position bearings to it every two minutes. Thus it was possible to return exactly to the spot where each target was recorded. The only target inspected in 1967 was that which we presumed might be the wreck of the Negro boy. A buoy was placed over the site and Don Rosencrantz and Yüksel Eğdemir descended along the buoy line in our two-man submarine Asherah, described in chapter 6. At 280 feet they radioed the surface that they had landed directly on top of a Roman wreck !

Time and weather did not allow, that summer, further inspection of the wreck nor of the targets in the 'Demeter' area. All of these were studied and photographed over closed-circuit television the following year by Laurence Joline and Frank Bartell. They spotted roof tiles, galley pottery, and what may be parts of broken bronzes among the cargo of amphoras. And two of the targets in the area of the 'Demeter' also proved to be wrecks, about 260 feet deep.

We will know definitely if we have found the wrecks for which we have searched so long only after each site has been examined thoroughly by divers wearing helium/oxygen equipment. But we have learned that a combination of side-scanning sonar and closed-circuit television provides the means of searching large areas of the sea-bed beyond the reach of ordinary divers.

4. DRAINING AND RAISING OPERATIONS

AFTER a successful survey is completed, the distinction between dry-land archaeology and underwater archaeology is often quite fine. A sunken ship, for example, may then be studied completely under water by divers. It may, on the other hand, be studied as a land site, either after the water has been drained or pumped from around it, or after its hull has been raised intact from the water. Variations on these approaches undoubtedly will be developed: mechanical hands, remotely controlled by television or mounted on submersible chambers or vehicles, will substitute for human hands, and air-filled domes constructed over submerged sites will act as complex coffer dams which have been pumped out. There will remain, however, only three broad avenues leading to the study of any underwater site: going under water to the site, removing the water from the site, or removing the site from the water.

All three approaches were followed in what was probably the first underwater archaeological venture ever begun, an undertaking started in the Renaissance but completed only in this century. Even variations on approaches were tried: the diving was done by breath-holding skin-divers, by helmeted divers connected to the surface, and by men in a diving bell.

The site was at the bottom of Lake Nemi, just seventeen miles southeast of Rome, where two Roman ships were traditionally said to lie. The legends which grew up around the ships were collected by Cardinal Colonna in the fifteenth century, and his interest led to the first attempt to salvage one of the ships in 1446, by the architect Leon Battista Alberti. First the ships were explored by swimmers brought from Genoa. Then Alberti built a raft of barrels, from which he ran ropes and hooks to the ship he hoped to raise. Attempts to pull the hulk ashore failed, but part of a large statue came up to arouse momentary curiosity and excitement.

Less than a century later, in 1535, the first archaeological reconnaissance with diving equipment was made. In fact, the diving suit worn by Francesco Demarchi in Lake Nemi may have been the earliest recorded for any kind of diving. Looking through a small crystal plate in his wooden helmet, Demarchi was surprised that everything was enlarged as he noted the brick paving on the deck of one of the ships, the hooks left in the hull by Alberti's efforts, and a number of anchors. He measured the ship and brought samples of wood to the surface, but his notes and most of his information were lost soon afterwards.

Skin-divers and a helmet diver had now inspected the ships, and attempts had been made to raise one. During the next exploration of the wrecks, in 1827, an eight-seat Halys diving bell was used. Annesio Fusconi, a hydraulic engineer, planted a huge barge over the site, partly to hold his bell and partly to hold the noted diplomats, scholars, and noblemen whom he had invited to watch his work. Even with elaborate equipment, however, Fusconi was frustrated in his attempts to raise one of the ships, as had been those before him. Many of the fragments of porphyry, marble, mosaics, metal columns, wood, and nails which he had retrieved were acquired later by the Vatican Museum.

Nothing more was done, except for some inaccurate measuring by a Flemish archaeologist, until 1895 when Eliseo Borghi, a private dealer in antiquities from Rome, came to Nemi with an amateur diver. They brought up bronze lion and wolf heads, as well as more pieces of mosaics, copper sheets, tiles and stone. From the two ships also came hundreds of feet of well-preserved wooden planks which were left to disintegrate on land. Finally the diving was stopped by the government, which had been forced to buy some of the objects from the dealer at exorbitant prices. At that time, Professor Emilio Gluria suggested that the ships could be saved by draining the lake, but no steps to implement such a project were taken. The idea was, however, revived under Mussolini, who decided that the Italian government should salvage what he glowingly described as 'immense and superb vessels, with rooms and gardens and fountains, ornamented with marbles and precious metals and rare woods, all shining with gold and purple'.

The surface of the lake was lowered more than 70 feet by enormous pumps which, starting in 1928, sent the water off into another lake lying at a lower level. When a substantial amount of the ship in shallower waters had emerged, after nearly a year, it became necessary to run the pumps more slowly. The hull was reinforced and supported against settling and coming apart as its liquid support receded, and it was covered with constantly sprayed canvas covers to prevent the wood from drying out too quickly and warping out of recognition. After four years, both ships stood in the open air and the pumps were stopped [Pl. 13].

The ships proved to be giants. One was 234 feet long and 66 feet wide, while the other was 239 feet by 78. They were sumptuously decorated, with mosaics and marble paving over their oak decks, bronze and marble columns in their superstructures, heated baths, and perhaps even cabins with shutter doors. Surely they were built for nobility, perhaps even for Caligula or Claudius, to whose time the ships have been dated by finds on board.

The value of the results has been controversial. Even while the work was in progress, an American archaeological journal reported that 'One of the ships has now been completely recovered, with results of the greatest value for the nautical techniques of the ancients, and for certain aspects of the arts and crafts.' At about the same time, the editor of one of the leading English archaeological journals found the results most disappointing : 'Three fine bronze animal-heads and a wooden hulk seem a poor return for so much expenditure.' An Italian answer to similar charges was that the results exceeded all expectations : 'The actual state of the first vessel . . . is by far nearer to its original condition than is the Forum today to the old Forum.'

Certainly the ships allowed archaeologists for the first time to inspect well-preserved hulls of the Roman period. Although built for a fresh-water lake, without shipworms, the ships had the protective sheathing of lead found on Roman sea-going vessels, indicating that the shipwrights had used normal building methods; the tenon construction was another indication that there was nothing exceptional about the hulls of these most unusual and lavish 'floating palaces'. A pair of sweep rudders showed that the ships were even meant to move about in the lake.

The long story of the Lake Nemi ships has an unhappy end.
The ships were burned by a group of German soldiers in 1944.
Now the museum by the lake holds only scale models, and
displays the objects found with the hulls.

Other archaeological discoveries made during drainage projects
have been mostly accidental. These include pile-dwellings un-
intentionally brought to light by the drainage of Swiss lakes, and
hundreds of boats found in the mud following operations to claim
new land in Holland. The remarkable discoveries made in the
Roskilde Fjord in Denmark, however, were the result of another
planned archaeological drainage programme.

The excavation of five Viking ships, which had been sunk nine
hundred years ago to block part of Roskilde Fjord against some
unknown enemy, began much like any other underwater operation. Scuba divers worked from a pontoon above the artificial
barrier of stones and sunken ships, and they used water jets and
suction hoses to clear away the mud. A wire, calibrated in metres,
was stretched across the area to serve as a base-line for plans
drawn with pencils on water- resistant paper.

Because of the poor visibility and a strong current, the leaders
of the excavation, Olaf Olsen and Ole Crumlin-Pedersen of the
National Museum in Copenhagen, decided that modified dry-land
techniques should be used; divers seldom wore their aqualungs
anyway, for the water was only one metre deep in many places.
In 1962, therefore, a sheet-steel coffer-dam was built to enclose
1,600 square yards of the site, and this area was gradually pumped
free of water [Pl. 15]. The enormous task, made possible by the
contracting engineers Christiani and Nielsen, and a number of
Danish foundations, removed the excavation from the realm of
strictly underwater archaeology.

As the Viking ships emerged into the air, their excavation
involved a mixture of land and underwater techniques [Pl. 16].
Dry excavators now worked from gang-planks over the fragile
wood, but final excavating and cleaning with 'spraying pistols'
was found to be more suitable than with the knives and brushes
of the land archaeologist. Once cleaned, the wrecks were mapped
photogrammetrically with stereophotographs, and then their timbers were marked, lifted, and wrapped in air-tight plastic bags.

The final stages of the excavation, like most of those under water, entail treating the wood with polyethylene glycol preceding eventual reconstruction and display in the beautiful new Roskilde Viking Ship Museum.

The work in Roskilde Fjord was begun as little more than an underwater training exercise, but its results were of surprising interest. According to Olsen and Crumlin-Pedersen, 'the five wrecks appear to be the remains not only of five ships but of five different types of ships: a light, a medium, and a heavy merchant vessel, a converted warship, and a "ferry" for the transport of persons in inland waters. By their variety and the excellent craftsmanship of their construction these vessels give a vivid impression of the scope of shipbuilding in the Viking Age.'

The excavation of the site illustrates the foolishness of trying to define 'underwater archaeology' precisely. Partly above and partly below water, the work falls mainly into the class of what has not yet, I am glad to say, been termed 'mud archaeology'. Such is also the case with the work of Peter Marsden on a Roman ship found in the mud of the Thames and excavated while enclosed by coffer-dams.

No less difficult to classify are the projects which raise ships and boats to the surface and sometimes remove them from the water altogether, where they may be studied in detail as if they were land finds. Only those wooden vessels which lie in fresh-water rivers and lakes, however, will normally be well enough preserved to be raised intact; elsewhere they will have been destroyed by shipworms shortly after sinking.

Three bateaux of the 1750s, raised from Lake George, New York, are the oldest boats recovered from American waters, except for some dug-out canoes that may be Indian. They were first seen by a diver wearing a home-made helmet cut from a hot-water tank to which air was sent from the surface by a hand-operated automobile pump. Fifteen or twenty years went by without further notice before they were spotted anew by a youngster who had just learned to dive. As has been so often the case, the diver began to destroy evidence in his own undisciplined exploration. A man trained in archaeology and methods of preservation was needed, and the Adirondack Museum's director, Robert Bruce Inverarity, was called to the scene and given the official permit to exploit the site.

Inverarity was the perfect choice for the job. He was already actively involved in research on the evolution of small boats in America, and he was particularly interested in the lightweight river boats known as bateaux. Not a diver himself, he acquired an underwater television camera which his divers trained on various relics so that he could observe them *in situ* and decide which were worthy of further effort. Only the flat bottoms of the thirty-foot boats were found, for wood exposed above the silt had been worn away by moving sand; but these could be raised from a depth of 30 feet by means of automobile inner tubes which were only slightly inflated on the lake bottom, the tubes rising gently as the air inside constantly expanded. An attempt to raise one of the boats with solid drums attached to steel bars placed under the old wood proved much too violent, and the entire float shot out of the water with destructive force.

Although the Roman ships in Lake Nemi and the Viking ships in Roskilde Fjord were certainly worthy of investigation because of their great age, the value of raising such comparatively recent boats as those in Lake George might seem questionable. Mere antiquity is not the only sign that unique knowledge is to be found in salvaged ships, however. At the Conference on Underwater Archaeology held by the Minnesota Historical Society in 1963, Inverarity pointed out why he raised these finds from the lake : 'No colonial bateaux have been preserved; there are only two known drawings in existence, and we are not certain whether they truly reflect colonial bateaux. So it becomes extremely important to determine the lines and the construction of these boats, which had a great deal to do with the whole growth of boat-building in America.'

Knowledge of a slightly later phase of American boat-building history has come from Lake Champlain, the scene of a valiant American stand against the British during the War of Independence. From his flagship *Royal Savage*, a seventy-ton schooner, Benedict Arnold commanded a total of fifteen vessels, most of them locally built galleys, against the larger, better armed, and better trained British fleet. It was October 1776, and the British were planning a drive which would split the colonies in half. The *Royal Savage* was damaged in the battle and, being less manoeuvrable than her oar-powered companions, ran aground on Valcour Island, where she was burned after dark by British troops. The gondola *Philadelphia* lasted throughout the day, but had been so badly hit that she sank from a hole near her bow shortly after the fighting ceased for the night. Arnold and his men were forced to retreat on land, after burning their fleet to prevent its falling into enemy hands, but by their solid resistance they had discouraged the British commander from continuing his plans. The battle was instrumental in saving the colonies from being cut in half from north to south.

Most of the *Royal Savage* above water had been blown away by the explosion of her magazine, but she could still be seen lying on the lake bottom in the 1860s. After numerous visits by souvenir hunters, her location was lost beneath the water until 1932. At that time Captain L. F. Hagglund, a department head of Merritt-Chapman and Scott, one of the leading American salvage firms, determined to find the historic relic. Local leads to its location were of little value, so Hagglund donned his helmeted diving dress and, with air pumped from a boat above, began to walk the bottom in ever-increasing circles. During his dives he found metal remains from the battle, but it was while rowing on the surface that he finally spotted the outline of the hull, about 20 feet under the calm water. Two years later, hearing that small boys had found the site and were beginning to rip the timbers apart, Hagglund returned during a vacation and trained a number of local inhabitants to tend his diving hose. Then he tried to determine if he really had found the *Royal Savage*. Robert Skerrett described this work the following year in the *U.S. Naval Institute Proceedings* :

'Accordingly, he patiently cleared away the mud within her afterbody and washed each bucketful for whatever might be hidden therein, and the same painstaking process was followed for some distance away on each side of the wreck. He was rewarded by thus recovering pewter buttons bearing the regimental symbols of troops known to have been at Crown Point and

Ticonderoga in the year of Arnold's naval service.' He also found pewter spoons, one engraved with the date '1776'.

There was no professional salvage equipment available for raising his find, so Hagglund improvised with empty tar drums which he tied to the hulk. With only one compressor to supply air to the bottom, he was forced to place the end of his one filling hose in each of the drums in turn, ascend, and change the air compressor from his helmet to the filling hose. Finally, after repeating this procedure for each of the twenty-two drums, the preserved portion of the hull was floated to the surface where it could be winched ashore. There each piece of wood was carefully marked before the hull was dismantled and placed in storage.

In 1935, Hagglund returned to Lake Champlain and succeeded in raising the much better preserved gondola *Philadelphia*, with her cannons and more than five hundred pieces of military equipment still inside. She now stands in the National Museum in Washington, with even the hole which sank her still clearly seen near her bow. Before she was raised, she had been known only from vague and hasty sketches.

The only gunboat preserved from the American Civil War came also from under water. She is the ironclad *Cairo*, raised from the bed of the Yazoo River in 1965 [Pl. 14]. One of the earliest ironclad warships in America, the *Cairo* has also the historical distinction of being the first ship ever sunk by an electrically detonated mine. She was sunk in 1862, near Vicksburg, Mississippi, by rebel-laid bottles of powder activated by copper wires running ashore. All of the ship's documents were lost but the sinking is vividly recalled by the cabin-boy's diary, which was saved. He wrote how the vessel had struck a torpedo at 11.30 a.m., how the hold began to fill with water in spite of the action of the pumps and how part of the deck was waist deep in water by the time another Union ship came to the rescue of the 160 men on board. The fifteen-year-old continued:

'We moved off just in time to escape being swallowed up in the seething cauldron of foaming waters. Nothing of the *Cairo* could be seen twelve minutes after the first explosion, excepting the tops of the smokestacks and the flagstaff from which still floated above the troubled waters the sacred banner of our country.'

Despite a number of efforts to salvage the vessel, the position of the *Cairo*, parts of her only 6 feet below the surface of the muddy water, was lost. Planks raised from the river in recent years were claimed as timbers from the gunboat, but Edwin C. Bearss, after studying all of the available documents on the sinking, concluded that they came from the wrong spot. Bearss, an historian for the National Park Service and a Civil War authority, joined forces with Warren Grabau, a government geologist, and M. D. Jacks, a riverman working for the Park Service, and the three of them set out down the Yazoo in Jacks' small boat in November 1956. They hoped to find the ironclad with a war-surplus compass as their only scientific instrument.

Once the needle of the compass wavered slightly, and the men marked a tree on the near-by shore to lead them back to the spot. But farther on, near the point that Bearss had reckoned the *Cairo* would be found, the needle swung around 180 degrees. Something magnetic was clearly affecting the compass, and it must be iron. Eagerly they shoved an iron rod down through the mud of the river bottom. The rod struck metal. They had re-located the *Cairo*.

Financial support for further work was not immediately forthcoming, but in 1959 two Mississippi scuba divers, Ken Parks and James Hart, offered their assistance. Working completely by feel, Parks and Hart buoyed key points on the vessel and cleaned a great deal of sand out of the pilot house with a water jet. From the pilot house the divers retrieved swords, a soap dish, a revolver, pitcher, wash-bowl, mirror, can of shoe polish, several bottles of medicine, a folding chair, a tub, and communications equipment. From the vessel's blacksmith shop came the anvil, vice, hammers, bits, and chisels. All remained as they had been a century before.

A large floating crane was lent to the operation in 1960 by the Anderson-Tully Lumber Company and, after a frustrating tale of stripping gears and breaking one-inch steel cables, the pilot-house was finally winched loose from the rest of the boat and brought to the surface. Such a structure had not been seen since shortly after the Civil War. Her sides of well-preserved oak were up to twenty-four inches thick, covered by plates of iron up to two and a half inches thick.

The pilot-house helped to spur the interest of the governor of Mississippi in 'Operation *Cairo*', and state support was obtained. U.S. Navy divers and a professional helmeted diver air-lifted mud from the ship's decks to lighten the load, and at the same time brought up guns and other artifacts [Pl. 1]. It was now proposed to raise the entire vessel with a pair of pontoons which would be attached to the hull while they were flooded; as the pontoons were pumped out, they would float higher in the water, raising the *Cairo* with them. This system as we shall see, worked with the raising of the *Vasa* in Stockholm Harbour, but the pontoons were pulled away from their moorings in the river and swept away by the current.

By 1965, a professional salvage company, headed by Captain W. J. Bisso, was called to the scene. Mud was removed from around the *Cairo* and seven steel cables, up to three inches thick, were worked under her hull. With four derricks, together able to lift more than one thousand tons, the *Cairo* was lifted from the river bed and carried upstream. A giant barge was placed in the hole left by the old gunboat in the mud, and the *Cairo* was carried back under water to be placed on top of the barge. But the water level had changed, and it was not possible to position the *Cairo* without raising her higher out of the water. The great weight of the 176–foot craft began to pull the heavy cables deeply into her sides, and attempts to raise her in one piece were abandoned. She was cut into three sections, and these were raised separately to be carried to a new museum in Vicksburg where she will be restored.

'Although it had been impossible to salvage the craft intact,' wrote Bearss for *Local History*, 'project sponsors had much to be thankful for. *Cairo* was like a huge time capsule, she contained thousands of artifacts, many of which cast new light on life aboard one of our country's first ironclads. Experts from the National Park Service and Smithsonian Institution have examined a number of items never seen before by people of our time. In the future anyone who writes about the river ironclads will have to come to Vicksburg to examine *Cairo*, for a study of the vessel has

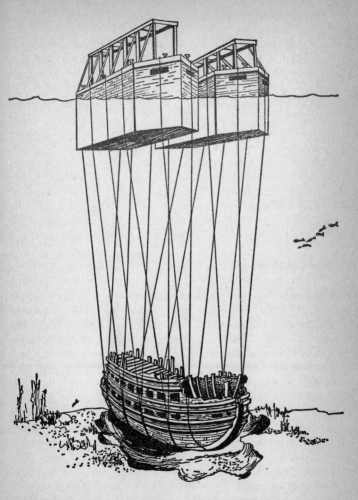

Figure 10. The V*asa* being raised from the bed of Stockholm
Harbour (after Anders Franzén)

revealed much about the craft's construction that one would never suspect from a study of documents.'

We have seen in Chapter 3 how another ship whose loss had been documented was discovered by Anders Franzén. Although not in a river or lake, the Vasa was protected against shipworms by the low salinity of the Baltic Sea, and Franzén was confident that the hull could be raised intact. Many ideas were proposed for her salvage, and Franzén has mentioned some of them: filling the hull with ping-pong balls, draining Stockholm Harbour, and freezing the water in the ship so that it would float to the surface as a block of ice which could then be melted. Wisely, more normal methods were chosen.

As in Lake Nemi, early work had been done from a diving bell. In 1664 another Swede, Hans Albrekt von Treileben, visited the ship in a bell and, in an incredible feat not fully understood, was able to raise about fifty huge guns from the hundred-foot depth. Now, between 1956 and 1959, helmeted Swedish Navy divers drove six tunnels under the wreck with powerful water jets. Their hoses were fitted with Zetterström nozzles which forced some of the water backward, equalizing the normal force which otherwise would have whipped them helplessly about. An air-lift carried the loosened mud to the surface. Working thus in absolute darkness, below the weight of hundreds of tons of ballast which might come crashing through the ancient hull once it was sapped, the heroic divers passed six-inch-thick wire cables through the tunnels and then over the decks of two great salvage pontoons on the surface above. The pontoons were then filled with water until their decks were level with the surface of the water in the harbour, the cables were pulled tight, and the pontoons were pumped out [Fig. 10]. As they floated upward, they lifted the seven hundred tons of the Vasa out of the mud. Then the pontoons, with the Vasa hanging below in its cable cradle, were towed to less deep water where the Vasa came to rest again. The Neptun Salvage Company repeated this procedure eighteen times, each time raising the ancient hull only the height of the pontoons. Finally, in 1961, the Vasa was near the surface. The last stage of the lifting was accomplished with hydraulic jacks so that the barges would not be pulled together, allowing the cables to cut through the wooden

Figure 11. Pewter gunpowder can, pewter tankard and wooden tankard from the *Vasa* (after Anders Franzén)

hull. Once on the surface, the *Vasa* was floated on her own bottom; divers had previously sealed every opening so that she was again 'seaworthy' [Pl. 12].

A permanent museum is now being built to house the *Vasa*, but already some of her finds have been preserved and displayed [Fig. 11]. A simple list here of the tools, weapons, eating and cooking utensils, and more than 4,000 coins would give little impression of the 'community in miniature' which had been revealed. Just one passage from C. O. Cederlund's catalogue of the collections will better convey a sense of the incredible finds from the early seventeenth century. Cederlund describes a dark-haired man, between thirty and thirty-five years old, whose body was found in the ship:

'The man's wearing apparel and the accessories he carried on his person were both well-preserved. He was dressed in a sweater of thick homespun cloth and full-cut, knit wool pants that were amply pleated at the waist and probably tied under the knees. Over the sweater he had a jacket with long arms and short, pleated tails. Under the sweater was a linen shirt. A pair of sandals and sewn linen stockings completed his dress. . . . A sheath with a bone or horn handle, and a leather coin purse were found at his waist. He apparently had some coins in a pants pocket as well. He had a total of about 20 øre or 2½ mark in copper coins altogether.'

As the *Vasa* is slowly treated with preservatives, the diving continues. Many of the details of the *Vasa*'s exterior had fallen off

long ago as the iron nails which held them in place corroded.
Beginning in 1963, divers began a search for these items which
are necessary for the restoration of the ship. Already more than a
thousand pieces have come to light, including nearly two hundred
additional sculptures and other ornaments [Pl. 8].

5. THE SALVAGING OF ARTIFACTS

Techniques of archaeological excavation on land are becoming increasingly refined, but it has not always been so. Just as many art treasures were pulled from the earth without regard for their stratigraphical context during the early days of 'archaeology', so many of the finest objects from beneath our seas and rivers were pulled up in nets and dredges, or by divers interested only in retrieving museum pieces. Most instances may be excused by the ignorance of those pioneers who first sought antiquities. Fortunately for underwater archaeology, it has sometimes been those guilty of the most brutal plundering who have realized their faults and have later introduced methods of scientific excavation. Even today, however, some underwater sites lend themselves to no more than salvage.

Stanley J. Olsen, a vertebrate palaeontologist with the Florida Geological Survey, has found more than mastodon bones in Florida's rivers. Swept into pockets in the river beds, with no chance of being *in situ* and even less chance of being meaningfully stratified, artifacts lie in an excellent state of preservation; these objects may aid greatly the study of fragments from similar pieces found elsewhere in stratigraphic context.

'Broken rum and wine bottles,' Olsen has written, 'are present at nearly every early 1800 military site in Florida. Complete bottles from such a locality are virtually unknown. However, from the soft silt and sand bottom of the St Marks River in north Florida several dozen complete green and black glass bottles [Fig. 12] have been recovered from an early nineteenth-century town site. Broken stems and bowls of white clay pipes are turned up by the hundreds in the screening of a dry excavation, but rarely is a complete pipe encountered. In less than six hours of diving I have collected more than thirty pipes, both white clay and glazed bowls, all from a depth of fifteen feet in one of Florida's swifter rivers [Fig. 13].'

Figure 12. Early nine-teenth-century bottles from the St Marks River in Florida (after Olsen)

The quantity of well preserved but scattered finds may be increased greatly if the objects have been put purposely under water. Sites which have so far defied thoughts of proper excavation, but which nevertheless have yielded unique hoards of artifacts, are the *cenotes*, or wells, of Mexico's Yucatan peninsula. The peninsula is formed of limestone which supports no surface rivers or streams of any note. The water seeps through the soft layers of stone, forming underground streams and hollowing out

Figure 13. Pipe bowls raised from a Florida river by S. J. Olsen (after Olsen)

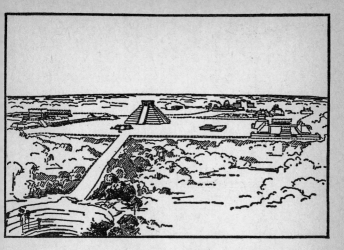

Figure 14. The *cenote* at Chichen Itza (Tatiana Proskouriakoff, courtesy Peabody Museum, Harvard University)

caverns. The roofs of some of the caverns finally collapse, forming open wells, or *cenotes*, whose walls are eroded until they sometimes are nearly perpendicular. The Maya Indians used some of the *cenotes* only as sources of water, but others they considered holy and used as sacrificial places.

The importance of the *cenote* at Chichen Itza [Fig 14] is indicated not only by its position at the end of a broad, paved avenue leading away from the city's major temple, but also by the meaning of the name of that great Maya capital: 'the mouth of the well of the Itza'. More specific knowledge comes from the Spaniard, Diego de Landa, who came to Yucatan less than sixty years after Columbus' discovery of the New World and died there a bishop in 1573. His *Relacion de las Cosas de Yucatan*, probably written in 1566 but not known to modern scholars until 1864, leaves no doubt as to the use of the *cenote*:

'Into this well, they have had, and then had, the custom of throwing men alive as a sacrifice to the gods, in time of drought, and they believed that they did not die though they never saw them again. They also threw into it a great many other things,

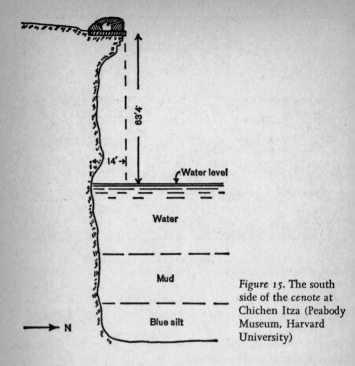

63'4"

14'

Water level

Water

Mud

Blue silt

N

Figure 15. The south side of the *cenote* at Chichen Itza (Peabody Museum, Harvard University)

like precious stones and things which they prized. And so if this country had possessed gold, it would be this well that would have the greater part of it, so great was the devotion which the Indians showed for it.'

We now know that from perhaps the beginning of the thirteenth century numerous men, women and children were led, accompanied by priests and musicians, to the edge of the well. With the priest offering prayers to the gods for rain or better times, the victims were cast into the water. A few, it was hoped, would return with word from the deities about future prospects, but it is doubtful whether many, if any, survived. Others were not expected to return; at some *cenotes* the victims were sacrificed before being thrown into the water. The best representation of such an act shows the poor soul held on his back while the

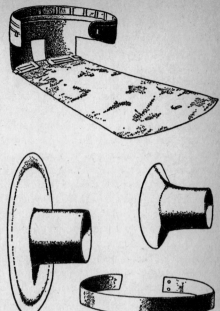

Figure 16.
Gilded copper sandal,
ear-plugs, and bracelet
from the *cenote* at
Chichen Itza (Peabody
Museum, Harvard
University)

priest cuts out his heart with a knife [Pl. 18]. The scene is pressed into a disc of sheet gold which was found in Chichen Itza's *cenote*. But it was only one of the spectacular finds from the salvage operations in this 'well of sacrifice'.

An early attempt to dredge the well in 1882, by the Frenchman Désiré Charnay, failed because of inadequate equipment. A dozen years later the site was purchased by Edward H. Thompson, a United States consul, and in 1904 he began the work which was to substantiate Landa's writings about it. Supported and directed by Charles Bowditch of Boston, he laboriously transported a derrick through the jungle and set it up with a boom which protruded nearly thirty feet out over the water of the well.

The *cenote* is roughly 164 to 200 feet in width, but Thompson made an arrangement whereby his metal dredging bucket could be lowered into any part of the well by ropes. The dredge dropped about 70 feet to the water from the edge of the *cenote*, and then passed through 35 feet of water and more than 35 feed of mud [Fig. 15]. After it was winched up by four men, visible objects were pulled from its steel jaws [Fig 16]. Then the remaining mud was dropped near the edge of the well and examined for smaller objects. Thompson had also learned deep-sea diving for the operation and he later suffered the common divers' complaint of impaired hearing from his own descents into the water and ooze; he was accompanied by two Greek sponge divers, unusual company for the jungle of Central America.

At the end of his campaigns, Thompson had done far more than simply prove the truth of Landa's writings. Alfred M. Tozzer, of Harvard University's Peabody Museum, where the artifacts were taken, wrote : 'There is perhaps no other single collection in New World archaeology that has offered so comprehensive a view of the aesthetic life of an ancient people.' Jade, carved in relief and in the round, was made into jewellery and human and animal figures. Copal and rubber were also used for figures at times, but some of it showed signs that it had been burned as incense during the sacrificial rites. Sheets of beaten gold included the disc with the sacrificial scene, as well as discs with scenes of battles on land and sea, and masks and plaques; there were also cast gold pendants in a wide variety of shapes. Hundreds of cast copper bells had been thrown into the well intact, unlike the jade and gold which had been ceremonially broken or crumpled in most instances.

As usual, the preservative qualities of water played an important role. Wooden sprinklers, rattles, and the handle of a sacrificial knife were among the ceremonial objects recovered, along with wooden spears, weaving tools, head-dresses, and other artifacts which would not normally be found in excavations. More than six hundred fragments of textiles have provided, according to Joy Mahler of the Peabody Museum, 'the only series of pre-Spanish fabrics which have survived in the Maya area. As such, they are a unique and extremely important source of our only technical information on fibres and weaving of the region.'

The discovery and study of sunken craft may one day throw new light on Maya coastal and riverine trade patterns; underwater archaeology already has been of value in the study of ancient Central American trade. The same limestone that produced the *cenotes* contains no metal or precious stones and, before the finds were made in the *cenote* at Chichen Itza, only three or four gold objects and a few copper objects had been discovered anywhere in Yucatan. The material from the *cenote* enabled S. K. Lothrop, also of the Peabody Museum, to trace the sources of various types of metal objects to such distant lands as Colombia, Panama, Honduras, Guatemala, and other parts of Mexico. Metallurgical and stylistic analyses of the material further allowed him to show that in some cases raw material was carried from one country to another, where it was fashioned into objects which were later carried by pilgrims or traders to Chichen Itza.

Thompson had raised an archaeological treasure which has, perhaps hastily, been compared to that of Tutankhamun, but much remained. Fifty-six years after the initial dredging, the Exploration and Water Sports Club of Mexico (C.E.D.A.M.) renewed operations, supported by the National Geographic Society in Washington and directed by the National Institute of Anthropology and History of Mexico. By this time the aqualung and the air-lift had become proven archaeological tools. Divers installed a large air-lift to suck mud from the bottom of the well and spew it out on a wire-screen strainer mounted between floats on the murky surface [Pl. 17]. More gold, jade, ceramics, fabrics, wood, rubber and some human bones came to light, as well as blocks of a temple which had fallen from the ledge above. In less than four months, more than 4,000 artifacts were recovered, and still more remained. In spite of this success, Pablo Bush Romero, President of C.E.D.A.M., decided that the work should stop until better methods of excavating can be devised. Stratigraphy has proved of little chronological importance so far, for the heavier objects simply sank deeper into the mud than the lighter, but the attitude of C.E.D.A.M. in their decision is commendable; technical advances may be able to untangle the jumbled context at a future date.

This was not the National Geographic Society's first venture into a Maya *cenote*. Only two years before, at near-by Dzibilchaltun, the Society's writer-photographer Luis Marden had led the diving part of a joint excavation with Tulane University. Here, at what is possibly the largest of all Maya cities, the diving was deeper and more dangerous [Fig. 17]. Coming up from more than 140 feet, on their third dive of the day, Marden and partner Bates Littlehales were both stricken with 'the bends'; a makeshift recompression chamber was of no use in their treatment, but they were saved from permanent paralysis by a speedily arranged U.S. Navy flight to a proper chamber in Florida. Their finds had again been staggering in volume. Thirty thousand pieces of pottery and other artifacts brought from the sloping side of the *cenote* presented enough possibly ceremonial objects to suggest that this well too had been used for more than a source of water [Fig. 18]. Among these were a flute, figurines, human bones, and, strangely, gorgonians or sea fans which grow only in coral waters and must have been brought to the *cenote* for some ritual purpose.

That such material, with its important bearing on Maya trade, technology and religion, could have been found only in *cenotes* where it had been cast is now evident. Less evident is the important role which similar underwater salvage operations have played in our knowledge of the history of Classical art. Today we know Greek sculpture too often only by Roman copies or literary descriptions. The vast majority of countless Greek statues have perished at the hands of man; bronzes were melted down for scrap, and marbles burned in kilns for lime. The earliest cult statues, the wooden figures known as xoana, have disappeared almost completely; three which remain, dating from the seventh or sixth century B.C., were found preserved in a sulphur spring in the territory of Palma di Montechiaro, Sicily. It is thus, under water, that we have our only hope of adding significantly to a growing catalogue of originals saved from destruction.

Until the recent discovery of a hoard of bronze statues near the harbour of Piraeus, there was but one large-scale bronze statue possibly dating from the Archaic period before the Persian destruction of the Acropolis in 480 B.C. This one exception, the Piombino Apollo, was netted by fishermen in 1812 off the coast of Etruria near ancient Populonia [Pl. 21]. Today it stands in the Louvre,

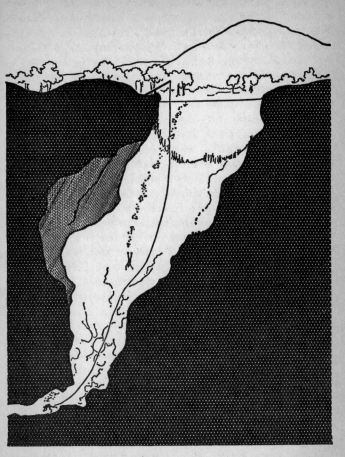

Figure 17. The *cenote* at Dzibilchaltun (after a *National Geographic* painting)

where at least one of the curators has considered it the prize of the *Salle des Bronzes*. Its dating, as is so often the case with such works, is controversial. If it is truly an original of the early fifth century B.C., it is one of the earliest Greek statues cast by the *cire perdu* process, the method still used for casting hollow bronzes. If, as has been suggested by Brunilde Ridgway of Bryn Mawr College, it is a first-century B.C. Roman creation, it remains unique; for it would show for the first time that the Romans were interested in copying Archaic Greek art, even to the point of adding an archaizing inscription in order to pass off the statue as a genuine antiquity. Did even the Roman collector need to be wary of unscrupulous dealers?

Between the time of the defeat of the Persians at Salamis (480 B.C.) and the administration of Pericles (449–29 B.C.), Greek art underwent the transition which would lead from the Archaic style into the Classical. Bronze overtook marble as the most popular medium for sculpture (a study of dedications from the Athenian Acropolis reveals pedestals for only three marble statues after the Battle of Salamis), and a master such as Myron, the greatest of the early Classical sculptors, could cast so skilfully that men and animals were said to believe at least one of his works was alive. Yet from the entire fifth century we have but two monumental bronze originals: the charioteer from Delphi, and the Poseidon or Zeus pulled from the sea near Cape Artemision in northern Euboea. The others we must be content to know through Roman copies.

One of these two originals, the Poseidon or Zeus [Pl. 19], may provide us with a work by Kalamis, one of Myron's most noteworthy contemporaries. The attribution is contested, but even the possibility would not exist save for underwater salvage. A Greek operation, sponsored by Alexander Benakis in 1928, raised the statue following the discovery of one of its arms by Greek sponge divers; a planned looting of the site by professional dealers luckily had been thwarted. But it was not the only bronze, for it was followed by a charming Hellenistic jockey and parts of a galloping horse. Pottery finds date the shipwreck to about the time of Christ, and pieces of the wooden hull indicate that the rest of the ship and its cargo still lie beneath the mud. What other treasures the ship was carrying we do not know. Shortly after one of the helmeted sponge divers had died of an embolism, as a result of rising too rapidly from 140 feet, the work was stopped.

The great masters of Greek sculpture during the second half

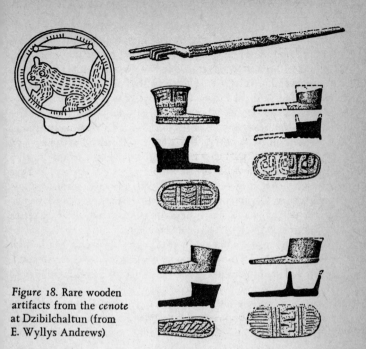

Figure 18. Rare wooden artifacts from the *cenote* at Dzibilchaltun (from E. Wyllys Andrews)

of the fifth century B.C. were Pheidias and Polykleitos, most of whose vanished works were also in bronze. We may recognize the genius of Pheidias, the artistic adviser for the great building projects under Pericles, in the sculptures of the Parthenon which were carved by artisans under his direction. Of his individual works, we have only Roman copies. Even here underwater salvage has played a small part. Pheidias' two major works were the huge ivory and gold cult statues of Zeus at Olympia, and of Athena in the Parthenon. Resting by the Athena, we know from literary descriptions, was a giant shield on which were depicted such scenes as a battle with Amazons which had supposedly taken place on the Acropolis. The scene was known by small Roman copies, but in 1930 a set of marble friezes came to light which presented the battle on about the same scale as it would have appeared on the shield, thus giving a much better idea of the style of the sculptor. At the same time, the rocks and walls of the Acropolis are seen clearly in the background, offering additional confirmation of the authenticity of the source of the scene. The copies had been dredged up, along with other commercial works of the second century A.D., from a flat-bottomed vessel which had burned and sunk in Piraeus Harbour. As in all of these salvage operations, we wonder what else may still lie beneath the mud.

The same dreary list of works long since disappeared continues into the fourth century, the time of Skopas, Praxiteles, and Lysippos. Skopas we know only from fragments of buildings on which he worked with other sculptors. Of Praxiteles we have only later copies, including almost certainly the marble Hermes discovered at Olympia, unless by 'rarest chance', as Rhys Carpenter has written, 'a bronze by Praxiteles has survived — as seems to be the case in the Boy from Marathon' [Pl. 20]. Until netted along with wood fragments in 1925, it had rested at the bottom of Marathon Bay, probably as only a small part of a cargo which awaits future exploration. Today it is one of the finest pieces in the National Museum of Greece.

Lysippos was the last of the great Classical Greek masters, a prodigal worker who made, according to Pliny, more than fifteen hundred statues. Yet, with one possible exception, we have not even a certain Roman copy to signify his work. This is the famed Youth from Antikythera [Pl. 22], thought by George Lippold to be a copy of an original by Lysippos, and, after further restoration in the Greek National Museum, tentatively attributed to the young Lysippos himself, by Vagn Poulsen, director of Copenhagen's Ny Carlsberg Glyptothek. It is the only extant large-scale bronze from the first quarter of the fourth century.

The Youth was only a part of an ancient cargo recovered off the tiny island of Antikythera, which lies south of the Greek mainland. The story of the discovery and exploitation of the site deserves a firm place in the history of underwater archaeology, for it was there for the first time in the Mediterranean that divers visited an ancient shipwreck and grappled with the problems of excavating it.

In the spring of 1900 a Greek sponge boat, returning from the sponge fields of North Africa, rode out a storm in the shelter of

Antikythera. Hoping to profit by the delay, one of the helmeted divers descended to look for sponges. Instead he found a field of partially buried bronze and marble figures, and he raised a larger-than-life-sized bronze arm as proof of his discovery. The captain of the sponge boat, Demetrios Kondos, went down to verify the story, and then sailed on to his native Syme to consult with others about the proper course of action. It was decided to approach the Greek authorities with the news – and the bronze arm – and soon an official salvage expedition was organized.

Plagued by bad weather, diving to the dangerous depth of 180 feet, the sponge-divers worked twice a day for five minutes at a time; even so, one diver died and two were permanently paralysed by 'the bends'. Their methods were primitive: moving clumsily about on the sea-bed, they groped in the sand and mud for objects which they tied to ropes to be hauled to the surface. More than once the rope broke, and the finds tumbled into deeper water where they could not be reached. No plans were attempted and never did any of the archaeologists on duty dive. With no photographs or drawings, we cannot imagine the appearance of the site, but the importance of the finds alone is great.

The Youth was not the only original bronze. A bearded head, thought possibly to be the portrait of a third-century B.C. philosopher, was brought to the surface along with a pair of fifth-century statuettes and a bronze bed decorated with animal heads. Fragments of other bronzes, probably including the draped body of the 'philosopher', were seen but not raised by Kondos' men. Less well preserved, in fact horribly eaten by sea animals, were thirty-six statues, thirty-three fragments of arms and legs, and four horses, all in marble. The marbles now lie in the courtyard of the National Archaeological Museum at Athens, where many of them have been identified as copies of original works, including the copy of a Herakles by Lysippos. They are important for our knowledge of the beginnings of exact copying techniques. The Roman fondness for, and acquisition of, Greek sculptures diminished the supply of originals to the point that copies were in great demand. The Antikythera marbles, originally destined for some Roman city, are, according to G. Roger Edwards of the University of Pennsylvania, 'among the earliest copies made by the pointing process whereby a faithful mechanical copy of an original at actual size or to scale could be made, earlier copies, less faithful having been produced only visually and freely.'

Not only students of ancient art have profited by the Antikythera wreck, but also students of the history of technology. A mechanism of gear wheels, dials, and plates was found in a badly corroded and encrusted condition. After the most delicate cleaning in the Greek National Museum, it was identified by Derek Price as a complex astronomical computer by which positions of the stars, sun, moon, and planets could be calculated. Price writes: 'Not only is this the only truly scientific instrument surviving from Classical times (with the exception of simple measuring devices, such as yardsticks and balances), but no literary allusions or texts would have led us to expect the existence in such times of any complicated mechanism of this character.'

Other small finds from Antikythera included beautiful glass vessels, a gold earring in the form of Eros playing a lyre, and the crew's tableware, storage jars, and lamps. Independent studies of such objects have led to a date of between 80 and 65 B.C. for the sinking of the ship, and such a precise date greatly increases the scientific value of the cargo. The citizens of Syme concerned with raising the cargo received the large sum of 150,000 drachmas from their government. Edwards continues: 'The bronze philosopher and Antikythera youth alone were worth their effort. Archaeologists interested in the studies of the various categories should, I am sure, feel equally grateful, for apart from the interest of the sculpture, the usefulness of the minor objects, being a group datable to a moment of time, is a thing of rare price, as any archaeologist knows.'

From the sea we have another fourth-century bronze original, the large, draped bust called Demeter now in the Izmir Archaeological Museum [Pl. 23]. Pulled up from nearly three hundred feet of water in sponge-dragger Ahmet Erbil's net, it lay on a beach near Bodrum until spotted by Classical scholar George Bean in 1953. The intensive search for the wreck which carried it has been described in Chapter III. Not only is it an exquisite piece, perhaps related to the British Museum's marble Demeter from near-by Knidos, but its drapery adds to its importance. An

Figure 19. Bronze figurine
of dancing dwarf from
Mahdia (after W. Fuchs)

understanding of the development of drapery styles is essential for
the correct dating of statues, yet our very scanty knowledge of
fourth-century drapery is gleaned mostly from reliefs and Roman
copies. As we have seen, most of our contemporary bronzes are
male nudes.

Another shipment containing Hellenistic works of art was lost
three miles from the Tunisian coast near Mahdia. Its story closely
parallels that of the Antikythera wreck. Both ships went down in
the first half of the first century B.C. (the Mahdia wreck is slightly
the earlier), both were found by Greek sponge divers in the opening decade of this century, and both provided vast quantities of
Greek works of art; five galleries of the Bardo Museum in Tunis
have been devoted to the display of finds from Mahdia. Both may

Figure 20. Bronze herm, signed by Boëthos of Chalcedon, from Mahdia (after W. Fuchs)

have been sailing for Italy, but the destination of the Mahdia ship remains in doubt and may have been North Africa.

Much of the Mahdia cargo remains beneath the waves, for it consisted of heavy architectural members, including bases, capitals, and more than sixty marble columns. The finest piece is a winged bronze Agon or Eros, but there were also bronze statuettes of dancing dwarfs [Fig. 19], Hermes, and a running satyr, as well as bronze fixtures for ornamenting furniture, and huge kraters and candelabra of bronze. A bronze herm [Fig. 20], by the Greek sculptor Boëthos of Chalcedon, provides a rare signed work of of the Hellenistic era. As usual there was found an abundance of terra-cotta vessels and lamps in a sealed and datable context.

From the marble statues, as from those found at Antikythera, we have valuable information concerning the beginnings of the techniques of copying sculpture by the pointing system. Here we have the suggestion that some original works were copied almost immediately after they had been made, perhaps even in the same workshops. The Agon, which seems to have leaned against the herm in a typical pose for marble statues which needed external supports, indicates further that marbles were now being copied in bronze as well as bronzes in marble. We may also assume because of the Greek inscriptions on board which had been taken from fourth-century temples in the Piraeus, that the ship had sailed from Athens. This led Alfred Merlin, director of the Mahdia salvage, to conclude that 'the authors of these copies had not, as has previously been imagined, emigrated to Italy, but that they remained in Greece and above all in Athens, whence right down to the last century of the Roman Republic were exported to the peninsula thousands of shiploads, such as ours, of statues, columns, sumptuous furniture and choice trinkets'.

During five seasons of three months each, between 1908 and 1913, salvage operations at Mahdia were conducted by the Tunisian Antiquities Department, then headed by Merlin. Even with government support and French naval assistance, the helmeted Greek and Turkish sponge divers faced the extreme difficulties of working in the open sea at a depth of 130 feet. But that was not the end of research on the wreck that was to play a second important role in the history of underwater archaeology. It was there, in 1948, that the French Undersea Research Group (G.E.R.S.), under Commanders Tailliez and Cousteau, made the first archaeological dives with their newly invented aqualungs. Still later, in 1954 and 1955, the Tunisian Club of Underseas Studies measured and mapped the site during the excavation and study of parts of the hull of the ship.

The list of isolated Classical antiquities from beneath all parts of the Mediterranean is long, and we can but mention a few of the other representative finds here. A second-century B.C. marble Aphrodite was pulled from the sea near Rhodes in 1929; four bronze portraits, including those of Homer and Sophocles, came from Livorno in the eighteenth century and were later placed in the Archaeological Museum in Florence; a four-foot-high bronze Poseidon, from the early fifth century B.C., was found in shallow water near Kreusis in Boeotia, where it had toppled from a shrine;

a bronze boy was taken from shallow water near Eleusis to Berlin; a Hellenistic bronze panther was raised from a first-century A.D. shipwreck near Monaco in 1949; a small bronze ship's ram recently appeared off the coast of North Africa; Greek helmets have been netted off the southern coast of Turkey; a Roman sarcophagus was raised in Spain; Roman bronzes of a Negro youth [Pl. 24] and the goddess Fortuna were dragged up in sponge nets off the south-west Turkish coast; and pottery and parts of anchors are constantly being discovered.

The Classical period is not alone, however, in its debt to underwater salvage. The Bronze and Iron Ages in the Mediterranean, and in Northern Europe as well, have also profited from chance finds.

In 1923 a cargo of bronze objects, including swords, spearheads, arrowheads, and fibulae, was dredged from what was probably a sunken ship in the Huelva estuary in Spain. These pieces seem to have been lost in the seventh century B.C., although many of the metal objects were already out of date and were being transported for their scrap value. The importance of the hoard lies in the variety of its objects and their parallels: the swords are similar to those of the Atlantic coast, as far as England, in the Late Bronze Age; the axes are similar to Sardinian examples; and the fibulae are like those of the Eastern Mediterranean. Thus we have not only evidence for far-flung relations at that time, but we are afforded a valuable synchronization between those distant areas. A Mediterranean-Atlantic trade route in the Late Bronze Age was further indicated to C. F. C. Hawkes, the well-known British authority, by a bronze axe of Sicilian type caught on a fisherman's line in Hampshire in 1937.

Remaining for a moment in the North, and turning through the pages of the *Proceedings of the Prehistoric Society*, we are surprised at how many examples used by J. D. Cowen in his studies of early bronze swords in Britain and Northern Europe were dredged from rivers: the Thames, Lea, Rhine, Saône, Weser, Nahe, Scheldt, and Seine. The same holds true for Sir Cyril Fox's study of socketed bronze sickles in the British Isles, and, to a lesser degree, for the studies of decorated bronze axes, and Bronze Age razors.

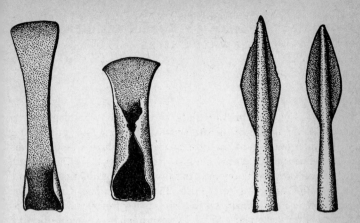

Figure 21. Bronzes from wreck near Béziers (after photographs courtesy A. Bouscaras)

What remains to be done by way of prehistoric archaeology under water can only be surmised. Pottery from every early period from the Early Bronze Age through the Iron Age has been netted in recent years off the coast of Israel. Earlier in this century Greek sponge divers stumbled upon a hoard of copper ingots in the Bay of Antalya on the southern Turkish coast, and other divers found a similar hoard while working on a new harbour for Kyme, in Euboea; the shapes of the ingots suggested that both hoards are earlier than that excavated at Cape Gelidonya (see pages 124–31) and date perhaps to the fifteenth century B.C. All of these potential sites are worthy of further investigation for the light they may shed on ancient trade.

At the time of writing, what may be one such early cargo in the sea off Béziers in France, is in process of being salvaged in a controlled and documented operation conducted by A. Bouscaras. No hull remains have been found, but already 760 metal tools, weapons, and ornaments, along with 600 kilograms of copper or bronze ingots, have been raised [Fig. 21]. The find has been dated tentatively to the eighth century B.C., and the completion of its study is eagerly awaited.

6. MAPPING AND RECORDING
UNDERWATER SITES

T HE primary duty of the field archaeologist is to record the details of his site before and during excavation. Thus his interpretation of the remains may be evaluated by those who will know the site only through its publication. Without plans, an excavation is no more than salvage. The techniques of recording differ according to the site: the same equipment is not used to map a huge Roman caravan city, sprawling over the desert, as is used to make plans of an Etruscan tomb or a Palaeolithic rock shelter. Nor are the same methods used on all underwater sites: size, clarity of water, and depth are all important factors to be considered.

Much is to be learned of larger sites by simple mapping, without excavation, where desert sands or sea-bottom mud have not completely covered the remains. Before Père Poidebard's study of the harbour-works of Tyre, between 1935 and 1937, the position, size and method of construction of that famous Phoenician port were unknown. Working before the invention of the aqualung, the French Jesuit mustered all the resources which his government could supply. Aerial photographs revealed the remains in shallow water. Helmeted divers, sometimes guided by a local skin-diver holding his breath, measured moles and took underwater photographs – the first made for archaeology – of masonry. The shallow depth allowed the placing of buoys on pertinent points, and these were plotted from the surface by ordinary surveying methods. Remarkably, Poidebard took stereophotographs through a glass-bottomed bucket held on the surface, and with these he was able to study the walls in three dimensions.

Apollonia, the port of the great Greek colony of Cyrene on the coast of Libya, was surveyed in 1958 and 1959 by a Cambridge University Expedition led by Nicholas Flemming. By that time the aqualung had been marketed in England for eight years, and the divers, mostly undergraduates, were able to swim freely over the remains. They took measurements with metre tapes strapped to their chests in reels, and drew and made notes on plastic sketch-boards. Again, the final plan was made by triangulating from a plane table on near-by land. Carrying copies of the preliminary sketches divers swam out into the harbour with surveyors' ranging-poles which they placed upright on predetermined points. Looking through the telescopic alidade on his plane table, their land-based partner sighted on the tips of the poles sticking above the water's surface and recorded the necessary vectors; up to thirty points were plotted, in turn, on a single dive. Details of masonry were measured and drawn under water. When they had finished, Flemming's group had made the first map of the great seaport which now lies half under water from either land subsidence or a rise in the sea level.

Caesarea in Israel, Sidon in Lebanon, Chersonesos in Crete, and Cherchel in Algeria are among the other ports which have been examined in varying detail since the introduction of free-diving. In general they have proved that previously made plans, based sometimes on literary descriptions, were incorrect. The French diver and writer Philippe Diolé, whose early reflections on the possibilities of aqualung archaeology showed great foresight, commented on the significance of Poidebard's work at Sidon and Tyre in establishing the importance of ancient ports: 'We know now what the size of a Roman colonial harbour in the second century A.D. really was. We are in a position to see what huge concrete constructions were used to protect the anchorage from incoming rollers, often at some distance from the land, how communication was established between a complex system of basins so designed as to accord with the traditional siting of a place which native experience had submitted to prolonged tests: different channels suited to different winds, the setting of store-houses, tanks and arsenals, the positioning of harbour-craft at the different quays. Sometimes, as at Sidon, there was an arrangement of flushes to prevent silting, taken over from the Phoenicians who had first installed it.'

The parts of ancient towns which once stood completely on land but are now submerged, either through sinking of the land or rising water levels, are not less important because they are under water. Not long ago such walls, towers, and roads were simply ignored by archaeologists. Now, with the relative simplicity of diving, joint land-sea surveys are becoming common. At Kenchreai, the ancient harbour town of Corinth, an expedition of the Universities of Chicago and Indiana has mapped the sunken walls and, in so doing, came across beautifully preserved mosaics and wooden furniture, as well as a variety of ivory mouldings and miniature architectural fragments. A Soviet team has recorded a tower and walls at what they believe is the ancient Greek city of Dioscuria; it now lies beneath the waters of Sukhumi Bay in the Eastern Black Sea. Joan du Plat Taylor, of the Institute of Archaeology of the University of London, has directed a group of diving archaeologists in the underwater phases of the excavation of Motya, a Phoenician port in Sicily. And Michael Jameson has now extended his mapping of the Peloponnesian town of Helieis out into its harbour. Only if such submerged elements are plotted can the plan of any ancient city be considered complete.

Sometimes an entire city has slid beneath the waves in a sudden geological upheaval. Such was the fate of Helike, which disappeared into the Gulf of Corinth during an earthquake in 373/2 B.C. For centuries afterwards, travellers wrote about the statues and other traces of the town which could be seen in the water. By now, however, the silting caused by nearby rivers may have covered the site with solid earth. Even if the city or part of it is still beyond the shore, it will be covered by so much mud that its mapping, which must precede any excavation, will be accomplished only by methods which will penetrate the mud. Core samplers could be of limited use at the risk of damaging valuable and perhaps unique artifacts. The near certainty that more original fourth-century B.C. works of art exist at Helike than at any previously excavated site, however, recommends the use of safe, mud-penetrating sonic devices which are being constantly improved. The Edgerton mud penetrator used in the port of Caesarea in 1963 was found by Elisha Linder, of the Underwater Archaeological Society of Israel, and Olivier Leenhardt, of the Monaco Oceanographic Museum, to be of help, but they felt that it should be used in conjunction with other instruments which physically penetrate the mud.

A sonic device has been used already in mapping the remains of another city which sank during an earthquake. Port Royal, once the pirate city centre of Jamaica and an important town for West Indian trade, was struck by a terrible earthquake on 7 June 1692, and two-thirds of the town slipped beneath the sea. Edwin A. Link, the noted aeronautical inventor, visited Port Royal in 1956 to see the remains of the catastrophe. Link's wife, Marion, described their disappointment for the National Geographic Society, which supported their later investigations:

'To our surprise, where these buildings once stood we could then find only a monotonous mud bottom under 20 to 40 feet of water, with never a sign of the old structures. When we had tried to dig into the bottom near Church Beacon with an inadequately small dredge, we penetrated four to six feet before finding a trace of the sunken town. Even the heavy brick walls of Fort James were hard to locate beneath the silt, with only a slight difference in depth and a crown of dead coral to mark their location.'

The Links determined to explore the old city and returned in 1959 with their marvellously fitted-out boat, the 91-foot *Sea Diver*, designed specifically for underwater archaeology. In order to know from which buildings they would be bringing objects to the surface, they made a preliminary map with an echo-sounder. Walls were spotted, marked with buoys, located by the navigator, and then plotted on an old chart of the city. Guided by the chart, divers retrieved objects from a fort, a cookhouse, and a ship chandlery [Pl. 26]. Hundreds of artifacts of copper, brass, pewter, iron, glass, and pottery came to light among the tumbled brick walls; even wood was well preserved by the layer of mud which seems to have covered the city as soon as it sank. Perhaps the most striking find was an encrusted watch which, when X-rayed, revealed the time at which it had been stopped forever by the earthquake.

Port Royal and other sunken cities and harbours cover many hundreds of square yards. The techniques used in their mapping would not necessarily be suitable on small, relatively flat sites which are easily covered with grids.

For generations, and probably even centuries, men have noticed the wooden piles which protrude from the shallow bottoms of lakes in southern Germany and Switzerland. The dates and purposes of some of these posts remained unknown, however, until the development of free-diving. In 1957 Gerhard Kapitän arrived at the little village of Altenhof on Lake Werbellin, where scholars fifty years earlier had reported the remains of some sort of lake-dwelling. Kapitän was determined to discover the exact nature of the site. With meagre equipment, unprotected against the cold water, and sometimes diving by merely holding their breaths, he and his friends made an accurate plan of the piles. They placed a wire grid, 25 metres square and divided into squares 5 metres by 5, over most of the site and fastened it down with wooden stakes driven into the flat lake bed. Each pile was plotted in relation to a grid-square with the aid of an aluminium measuring rod, and the position was recorded on an aluminium drawing board; the pictures drawn under water were transferred to a scaled plan following each dive. The finished plan indicated a nearly square structure in the lake, enclosed on one side by a curved row of piles, while farther out in the water were three double-rows of piles which had supported another structure.

Professor P. Grimms believed that Kapitän's plan was that of a medieval stronghold, and a trial trench dug at his suggestion on the facing shore revealed numerous potsherds of the thirteenth and fourteenth centuries. Further diving, in 1958 and 1959, turned up similar pottery and other contemporary artifacts, including part of a silver cup, among the piles themselves. The date makes it almost certain that the settlement was a place of refuge built by a robber-knight, for contemporary documents mention the construction of such places in open water. Local legends of castles sinking into various lakes probably reflect the destruction of these pile-strongholds by armies sent against the robber-knights.

In 1960, for the Deutsche Akademie der Wissenschaft of Berlin, Kapitän mapped the remains of a similar lake-dwelling. It lay less than seven feet deep in the Cambser See, in the province of Schwerin, Germany. The previous year he had been shown the site by fishermen, and had studied its layout from a boat on the surface after having marked more than fifty of the piles with crude little buoys. Now he and his assistants cleaned away the vegetation that covered much of the area, and marked the corners of the site with buoys for the placing of the grid. This grid was smaller than that used before: a square, 10 metres by 10, subdivided by copper wires only 2 metres apart; a fixed diagonal strip insured that the grid would be stretched out into a true square once on the bottom. The divers, using pencils, marked the positions of posts on reduced grids carried on drawing boards; these drawings were photographed after each dive. Positions of posts outside the grid were taken with a metre tape, and positions of objects excavated from the muddy bottom were recorded not only by the drawings but by underwater photographs [Fig. 22].

The results of the work present a structure about 9 metres by 9½ in area, probably linked to the shore by a foot-bridge resting on piles. Among a large number of stones, many of them flat, which had fallen from the dwelling, were signs of burning which suggest a hearth. That the entire structure had burned, however, was indicated by burned masses of mud wall plaster and burned wooden planks. The pottery, found with knives, cross-bow arrows, door-hinges, nails, animal bones, and other miscellanea in the mud below, again points to a fourteenth-century date. Only through underwater archaeology could the mystery of these particular lake-dwellings have been solved.

Accurate plans and sections of ancient shipwrecks are as important as those of inundated habitation sites. Only through such records will we learn how ships were constructed and laded in various periods of antiquity. Even the stratigraphy of a cargo may be of importance for, as on land, *upper* generally means *later*. If a wreck is found with Syrian goods piled on top of Egyptian goods, we have the probability that the cargo carrier had stopped in Syria after visiting Egypt. Thus we learn something about the course of that particular ship, which adds a little to our general knowledge of trade routes of the past.

There is also the possibility that more than one wreck is involved at a site, one on top of the other, and only accurate records can sort out the items of their mixed cargoes. Scattered over the treacherous reef at Yassi Ada in Turkey, as has been mentioned, Ottoman cannon balls are mixed with Roman amphoras, while a hundred yards away, in 120 to 150 feet of water, three well-

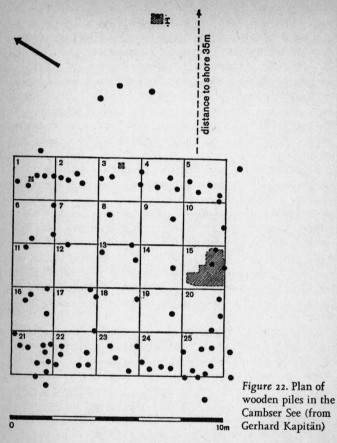

distance to shore 35m

Figure 22. Plan of wooden piles in the Cambser See (from Gerhard Kapitän)

preserved wrecks of different dates lie within fifty feet of one another; not only had a 16th-century ship settled partly on top of a Roman ship, but its galley had landed directly over the Roman ship's galley, mixing their coins and pottery together in a two-metre square area of the sea-bed! Off the Sicilian coast not far from Syracuse, Piero Gargallo has seen a spot where a modern tanker, a nineteenth-century sailing ship, a medieval ship, and a Roman merchantman all lie together.

It is obvious that if a point is dangerous enough to sink one ship, then it is likely to cause the sinking of a second. The importance of this conclusion is well illustrated by the work at Grand Congloué near Marseilles. That famous excavation of a Roman merchant ship, the first undertaken by divers with aqualungs, opened the way for scientific underwater archaeology. Good mapping methods were not, however, developed during more than five years of digging, with the result that only a dotted oval line represents the ship and its cargo in the scientific publication of the site. From this vague area thousands of pieces of pottery were raised to the surface. Some experts believe that many pieces from the upper levels at Grand Congloué are a century younger than those from the lower levels. This would indicate that two wrecks are involved, one having settled on top of the other; the wood of the upper ship, held out of the protective mud and sand by the earlier cargo below, would have soon vanished; but the pottery cargo would have spilled over and covered that below. The divers deny this theory, but they kept no records to settle the dispute one way or the other. Thus the cargo which should represent the contents of a closed and datable deposit, one of the greatest benefits shipwrecks offer archaeology, has lost its main scientific value.

Since the Grand Congloué excavation, many mapping techniques have been used. Of the methods of taking planimetric measurements on shipwrecks, triangulation by metre tapes is one of the cheapest and least complicated for sites too large to be covered easily with a grid. Control points, at known distances from one another, are first selected and marked on the sea-bed around the site [Pl. 25]. Horizontal measurements from two of these markers to any object or point on the site provide the information necessary for plotting the position of that point on a plan. The advantage of triangulation is that it may be done effectively by small teams of divers, with little equipment, especially on level, uncomplicated sites. Further, extremely clear water is not essential. The method is quite time-consuming, however, and proves uneconomical on sites at great depths where limited diving time is such an important factor. On a wreck at Cape Spitha in Greece, for example, Peter Throckmorton's divers recorded over fourteen hundred measurements; luckily the survey was in only thirty feet of water.

The wreck at Cape Spitha, near Methone in the southwestern Peloponnesus, consisted of huge granite columns and column fragments spread over an area about 100 feet long and 65 feet wide. None of the hull of the ship was preserved, as is usually the case on shallow wrecks which suffer from wave action, and even heavy cargo had been moved about. Throckmorton and his group, working under the auspices of the Hellenic Federation of Underwater Activities, 'decided that the only practical way of recording and studying the site was by drawing a carefully measured plan. The area was too large to be encompassed by a single photograph, and, because of distortion under water, a mosaic photograph would have been inaccurate. There were peculiarities in the lengths and shapes of the columns which could be understood only by studying a plan based on precise measurements' [Pl. 27].

The last statement is important, for the underwater archaeologist can often 'see' his site only on paper. On land I have spent hours on a high photographic tower, trying to understand better the walls and houses I had just excavated below; all around I could see the other trenches and remains of the entire prehistoric mound, and in the distance the mountains and water which made up the landscape stood out clearly. Even the largest land site may be seen as a whole from the air. The diver's view of his site, on the other hand, is often limited to small areas at any one time so that he never gets a complete view of it at once.

The plan made at Cape Spitha was the first ever of an underwater archaeological site in Greece [Fig. 23]. It allowed the surveyors to calculate the weight of the cargo as 131.50 metric tons, which could be carried comfortably in a sailing vessel 100 to 130 feet long. The plan also revealed that the columns were from a building already destroyed in antiquity. The fragments could not be fitted together, proving that they had not been broken during the sinking of the ship. Thus the columns came neither freshly from a quarry nor from a standing building. Presumably the missing pieces were in another ship. An explanation for this medieval shipment of late Roman column fragments may come from further investigation of the site.

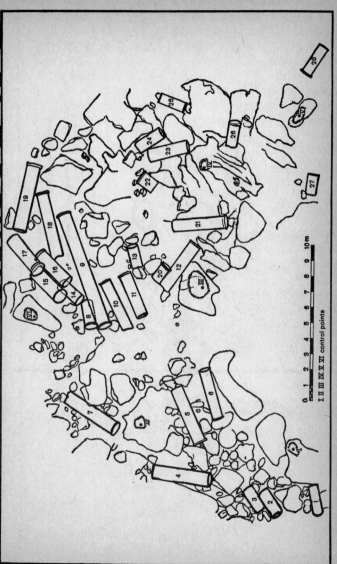

Figure 23. Cargo of granite colums at Cape Spitha, near Methone (from P. Throckmorton and J. Bullitt)

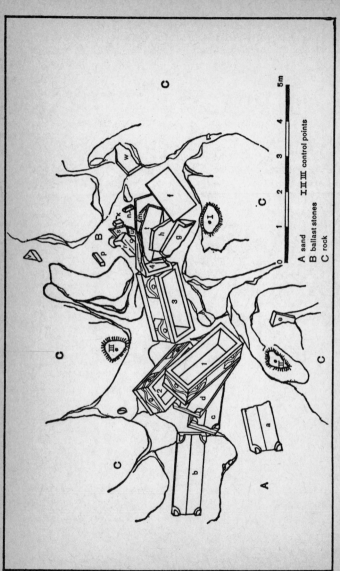

A sand   I II III control points
B ballast stones
C rock

0   1   2   3   4   5m

Figure 24. Cargo of Roman sarcophagi at Cape Spitha (from Throckmorton and Bullitt)

Not far from the column wreck, one of its surveyors, Nikos Kartelias, accidentally discovered four granite sarcophagi with lids [Fig. 24]. Ballast stones and roof-tile fragments with the sarcophagi indicated to Throckmorton that this was another ship-wreck site, although again the depth had not allowed the pre-servation of any hull remains. A glass vessel found on the site dates the wreck to the second or third century A.D.

Simply recording the cargo, without raising any of it, was im-portant for the study of the Roman marble trade; this trade John Ward-Perkins of the British School in Rome has referred to in a letter to the director of the University Museum, Philadelphia, as 'one of the most promising fields open to the underwater archae-ologist'. Ward-Perkins' intensive study of Roman commerce in marbles, granites, and porphyries lends authority to his sub-stantiation of that statement: 'The literary and epigraphic docu-ments, the quarries and marble yards, the buildings themselves and the sculptures, all of these can tell us something about this important commerce, but for a great many of the details we badly need the evidence of actual shipments. We know, for example, that many items such as columns and sarcophagi were regularly shipped partly prefabricated. But to what extent were the column-dimensions standardized? Were the Attic sarcophagi partly carved before despatch? Were capitals and bases ever shipped in the rough? What qualities of marble might be associated during ship-ment? These are a few only of the questions that may expect an answer from the location and study of wrecks; and conversely, since the sources of the marble are mostly known and the mar-kets which they served often very specialized, the wrecks of marble ships should be one of the most profitable sources of information about ancient shipping and shipping routes.'

The photographs and drawings made by Throckmorton at Cape Spitha showed that raised garlands on the sarcophagi had been only blocked out; the detailed carving of petals and leaves remained for a craftsman to carry out at the destination [Pl. 28]. Some of Ward-Perkins' questions were being answered – and since that time he and Throckmorton fittingly joined forces on another lost cargo of sarcophagi near Taranto in Italy.

Triangulation provides only horizontal measurements, and

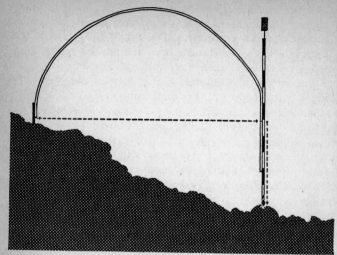

Figure 25a. Method of measuring relative elevations with a piece of transparent plastic hose; when bubbles appear at the end tied to a bench mark, the air-water interface at the other end of the hose will be at the same level

elevation measurements are needed for drawing sections of wrecks and their cargoes. A simple method of determining relative elevations, with a range pole and levelling device, was demonstrated by Donald Rosencrantz during the University of Pennsylvania Museum's survey of a fourth-century A.D. wreck lying in 140 feet of water near Yassi Ada, Turkey [Fig. 25]. Paul Merifield, expedition geologist, describes the process: 'A light-weight, graduated metal rod two metres long served as a range pole; this was made neutrally buoyant by a small float attached to one end. A transparent plastic hose one centimetre in diameter and ten metres long provided an ideal level. A diver blowing into one end of the hose filled it almost entirely with air, and the air-water interface within the hose was held at the highest point on the wreck. The hose, buoyed up by the entrapped air, formed a broad convex-upward arc, and a second diver held the opposite end of the hose against the range pole, which rested vertically atop a nearby amphora. The position of the air-water interface on the range pole

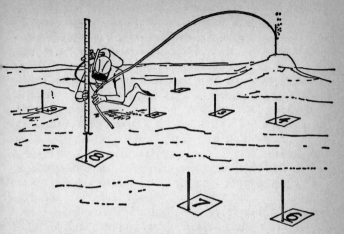

Figure 25b. The apparatus in use (drawing by Vince Malcolm)

indicated the difference in elevation between the two points. A third diver recorded the reading and directed the movement of the divers. Each measurement consumed an average of two minutes. After all desired points within reach of the hose had been measured, the first diver moved to a point just measured that bordered the unmeasured points, and new points were measured relative to this one.'

A more recent instrument, the differential depth gauge, was invented by diver-engineer Robert Love to measure relative elevations of artifacts sunk at 'Site X' in the Galli Islands off the Italian coast [Pl. 30]. He describes the instrument as follows: 'The case of a small Bourdon pressure gauge is sealed and filled with oil. A compressible bellows, also oil-filled, is attached to the case and connected to the interior of the case so that external pressure on the bellows is applied to the outside of the Bourdon tube. The normal gauge inlet to the inside of the Bourdon tube is connected via any required length of 4 mm. plastic hose to a reference chamber, in this case a rubber inner tube, which also senses water pressure. The Bourdon gauge thus responds to the difference in water pressure sensed by the reference chamber and the bellows.

'In use the reference chamber is anchored above the wreck site with the connecting hose free to allow a diver to take the gauge to various points of interest. When placed on each point, the gauge indicates the depth below the reference chamber. The diver is free to move to various objects and needs only seconds to record gauge readings. The one-atmosphere vacuum range of the differential depth gauge built for Site X represents a full scale of approximately 10 metres in depth below the reference chamber. Relative elevations read with this gauge are accurate to within 12 centimetres and are independent of surface tidal changes. The 20-metre length of plastic hose used here floats free of the bottom entanglements. Longer hose lengths and more accurate elevation readings are possible using instruments built along this principle.'

Using such a gauge, Love and his group were able to make one of the most accurate survey maps of any underwater site. Their plans enabled them to conclude that the 27 Graeco-Roman anchors found at Site X were from three separate ships of the same period. Further analyses of the artifacts and continued study of the site, already planned, will, it is hoped, tell us the date and cause of this hoard of Classical anchors, the largest ever found.

What may be a more efficient method than triangulation of obtaining planimetric measurements is being used successfully by Mendel Peterson of the Smithsonian Institution during his work in the Caribbean [Pl. 31]. A wheel with degrees marked on its rim is mounted on a shaft which Peterson drives vertically into each site. A metre tape pulled out from the top of the shaft measures the distance to any point, and the direction may be read on the wheel where it is crossed by the tape. A slightly larger wheel, mounted over and perpendicular to the first so that it could pivot around it, would allow elevations to be calculated from simultaneous readings of upward or downward angles. At present Peterson is able to determine elevations, including curvatures of wooden hull members, by means of a horizontal pole, set up on a stand, from which numerous vertical rods may be dropped onto the site and locked in place [Fig. 26].

Another method of plotting points in three dimensions under water has been devised independently by Frederic Dumas and by Italian archaeologists. Dumas' version was used successfully during the University of Pennsylvania's first season of excavation on

②

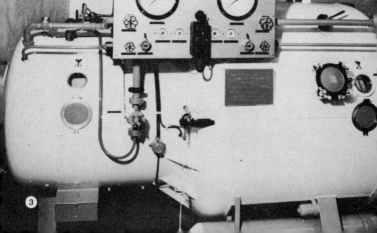

③

5

6

8

9

10

18

19

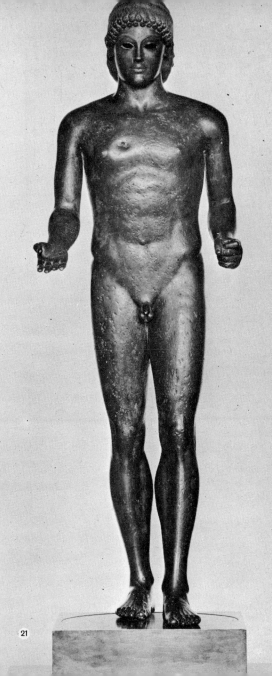

23

24

25

26

31

32

33

34

35 36

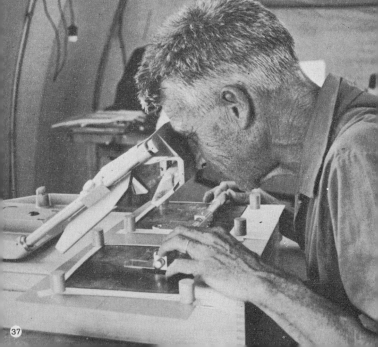

37

41

42

43

44

45

54

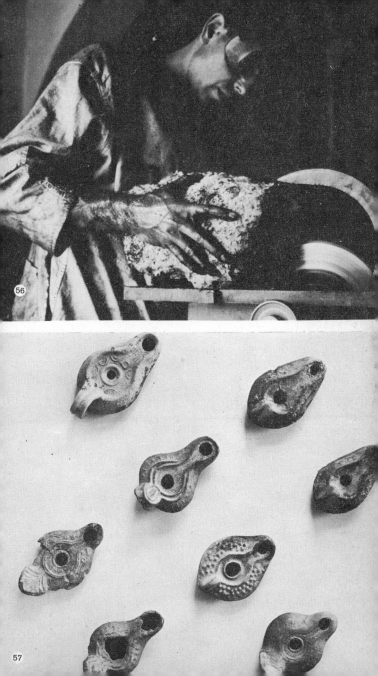

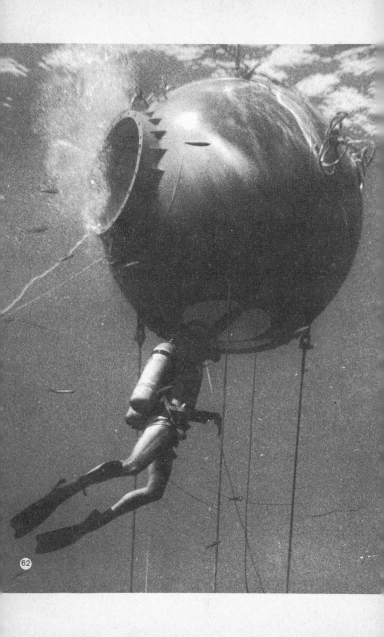

the Byzantine shipwreck at Yassi Ada [Fig. 41]. A 5 metre-
square metal frame, calibrated in centimetres, was placed over
part of the site and levelled horizontally on four telescopic legs.
Riding across the frame, as if on tracks, was a beam which also
was marked in centimetres. A calibrated vertical pole was yoked
to the beam. It was possible, therefore, to place the bottom of the
pole on any point within the frame, and to read the coordinates
of that point on the sides of the frame and the beam, and the
elevation on the pole. These figures enabled the architect to place
the points on his plan, but details around the points had to be
drawn by artists hovering over portable wire grids placed over
the wreck. As in all of the systems described, it was necessary to
clean the site of undergrowth and to tag all visible objects with
identifying labels, usually numbered plastic tags on wires, before
beginning the plotting.

In clear water, plane tables may be used as on land, both for
triangulation and for taking elevations [Pl. 32, Fig. 27]. Two tables
are placed a known distance apart on the sea-bed. A diver pins
a sheet of frosted plastic on the horizontal top of each table and

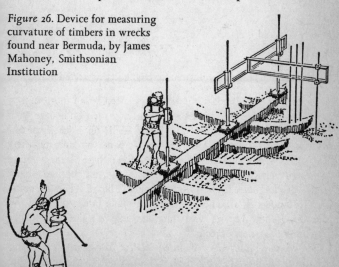

Figure 26. Device for measuring
curvature of timbers in wrecks
found near Bermuda, by James
Mahoney, Smithsonian
Institution

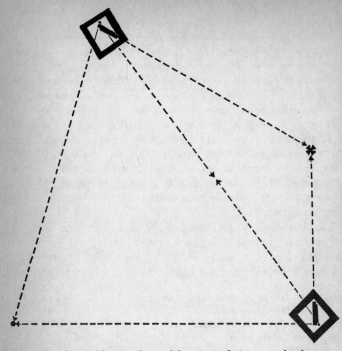

Figure 27. Plane tables may be used for triangulation as on land

places on top of this his sight; the sight need be no more than a piece of pipe fitted with cross-wires and mounted on a base with a straight edge on one side. The divers sight on a fixed control point and then draw lines on the plastic paper by running their pencils along the sight bases. A third diver then places a range pole, kept vertical by a small float on its top, on the first object or point to be plotted. He notes on a sketch board what the point is and numbers it '1'. The divers at the plane tables sight on the pole, draw their vectors, and number these '1'. The pole-tender then moves to a new object.

One of the tables may be used as the base-point for taking elevations on the site [Fig. 28]. For each point, the plane-table operator signals the pole-tender to move his hand up the calibrated

Figure 28. Method of measuring relative elevations with a plane table

surveying pole until it is level with the horizontal element of his cross-hairs. He then signals for the hand to stop, and the pole-tender records the elevation from the pole. If the water is some-what murky, a flashlight held by the pole-tender would aid each step of the operation.

Plane tables, first used during the excavation of the Byzantine shipwreck at Yassi Ada and later employed on the two wrecks near Methone in Greece, have the advantages of being extremely inexpensive, for the components can be made of handy scraps of wood and pipe, and being useful on very uneven bottoms. Their use depends on clear water, however, and since they require the work of several divers at a time, they are quite time-consuming to operate.

So far we have mentioned ways of plotting points, but plans consisting simply of points would be meaningless. The details of cargoes and hulls may be drawn with the assistance of photo-mosaics, made of overlapping vertical photographs, which have successfully aided underwater map-making on many sites in the Mediterranean since first made by Philippe Tailliez of the Titan wreck in France. A bull's-eye level and a plumb line attached to a camera insure that the photographer swims at a fixed distance over the sea-bed and holds the camera perfectly level. Horizontal metre sticks, laid previously over the site, allow the resultant negatives to be enlarged to the same scale. Many published mosaics, unfortunately, look like crazy quilts. They are too dependent on the photographer's ability to swim a set course, even in a current. To insure complete coverage, Nino Lamboglia and Gianni Roghi laid down guide lines on their site at Spargi.

Spargi is a small island just north of Sardinia; there an amphora carrier sank in 55 to 60 feet of water between 120 and 100 B.C. [Fig. 29]. A grid system of yellow canvas tape, attached to wooden stakes, divided the wreck into two-metre squares during the first phases of its mapping; the tape grid was later replaced by a rigid system of horizontal pipes on legs. Each of the squares was photographed separately by a diver, but even with these guides, Roghi reported, 'photographic planning is the most exhausting job for a diver to carry out, particularly if he is disturbed by the current.' It was also found that necessary detail could not be obtained if the camera was more than 3 metres above the wreck. Lastly, Lamboglia added, the photographs produced a plan, but did not provide the necessary information for drawing sections.

The shortcomings mentioned by Roghi and Lamboglia were later overcome with an adaptation of their system used by the University of Pennsylvania Museum in its mapping of the Byzantine shipwreck, in 120 feet of water, at Yassi Ada, Turkey [Pl. 54]. Divers first constructed an angle-iron scaffolding over most of the site. This was in the form of nine rectangular frames, each 6 metres by 2, which formed steps running up the slope on which the wreck lay. Each step was placed as close as possible to the sea-bed, levelled, and then fixed firmly to its six pipe legs by means of thumbscrews; metal plates prevented the pipes from sinking far into the sea-bed, but a constant check on the level of the steps indicated that the plates should have been larger.

Resting on the horizontal steps were a pair of 4 metre-high photographic towers of light metal. Each tower had a base 2 metres square, made into a grid by tightly stretched elastic cords 20 centimetres apart. In this way the nine step-frames, each broken into three 2-metre-square sections by wooden dividers, provided twenty-seven fixed positions for the easily moved photo-towers. The progress of excavation in every area was, therefore, recorded with grid photographs taken with a Rolleimarin camera through holes in the tops of the towers.

The photographs, thus taken from a firm platform, were of ex-cellent quality, but they could not be traced directly onto the over-all plan of the site. Differences in scale between higher and lower objects needed correction, by computation or optical pro-jector, once the relative elevations of the objects were known.

Figure 29. One of the earliest methods for systematic mapping of an ancient wreck; Spargi (after Roghi)

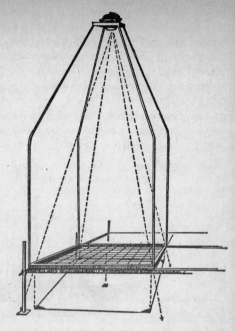

Figure 30. Only objects in the centre of each photograph taken from the photo-tower will be seen properly related to the grid; positions of others must be corrected

The elevation measurements were taken with a weighted metre tape dropped like a plumb line from the horizontal grid cords [Pl. 34].

A second necessary correction was more time-consuming. In each photograph the only object seen in true relation to the grid above it was that in the centre of the picture [Fig. 30]. All of the grid photographs had to be redrawn, therefore, with positions of objects being moved according to their distances below the grids and their lateral distances from the centres of the grids. The third possible source of error, the 'pillowing' effect in photographs taken under water with ordinary lenses, was easily corrected by means of the grid lines in each picture.

Photo-mosaics of all types depend on clear water. They may be made in muddy water, however, by mounting the camera at the top of a cone which is the same height as the desired height of the camera above the site. The base of the cone can be covered

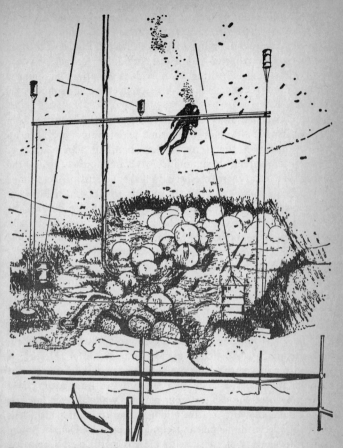

Figure 31. Method of taking stereophotographs at Yassi Ada

with a flexible sheet of transparent plastic. The cone is pumped full of clear water while submerged. As the cone is moved over the sea-bed, its plastic base moulds itself over the various contours and objects, minimizing the amount of muddy water between the object and the camera above; the photographs are taken, therefore, through virtually clear water.

At Yassi Ada, luckily, the water was extremely clear, and the stepped scaffolding produced plans as accurate as those made on land excavations. It had, however, serious disadvantages. The mere erection and levelling of such a structure at depths from 100 to 150 feet, requires the use of many divers for many days or even weeks. The measuring of individual elevations by hand is laborious and time-consuming. A better method of mapping was needed.

The University of Pennsylvania Museum's underwater team realized in 1962 that most of its time under water was taken up with mapping. A simple method of obtaining planimetric and elevation measurements simultaneously would greatly reduce the diving time on any wreck, especially if the measurements could be taken by only one diver. As far back as 1958, Dimitri Rebikoff, the noted underwater photography specialist, had published the suggestion that wrecks could be mapped photogrammetrically with stereo-photographs, but no one had yet attempted it. Simple experiments in underwater stereo-photogrammetry began finally at Yassi Ada in 1963, with Julian Whittlesey, whose city planning firm had been involved in aerial surveys, acting as an adviser for the programme.

A horizontal bar was floated about 6 metres above one end of the Byzantine shipwreck [Fig. 31]. The bar was notched every 1.20 metres. A Rolleimarin camera hung from the bar on gimbals, and was weighted so that it always remained level [Pl. 33]. A single diver moved the camera along the bar, taking a picture at each of the notches; a cable release improvised from a jeep choke cable prevented the camera from moving while the picture was being taken, allowing relatively long exposures with a small lens opening. Special development techniques used by Donald Rosencrantz, formerly a physicist with the Eastman Kodak Company, produced pictures which, taken with natural light, showed clearly even the numbers on the plastic identification labels tied to amphoras more than 25 feet below. A noted oceanographer with many years of experience later called the pictures the clearest ever taken under such conditions, indicating that the limits of underwater photography cited in most books on the subject had been unduly narrow.

The photographs taken as described formed a series of stereo-pairs which presented the wreck in three dimensions when seen under a stereo-viewer [Pl. 35–37]. More important, the parallax in the pairs could be measured with a micrometer, and the elevation of any object then calculated by the simple formula :

$$\frac{f \times b}{p} = H$$

where f is the focal length of the lens, b (base) the distance between cameras, p the parallax, and H (height) the distance from cameras to object.

The desired figure, the distance from cameras to object, is the only unknown factor and is easily obtained. Only one camera was used at Yassi Ada, so the distance between cameras was the 1.20 metres between camera positions on the bar.

The results were encouraging but not perfect. The distortion caused by the difference between the index of refraction of water and that of air (exemplified by the apparent 'bending' of a stick half in and half out of water) caused errors if direct measurements were made from the photographs; displacement of a point by only 1 millimetre on the photographs would cause an error of 7 centimetres in the elevation reading on that point. The problem was later solved by the addition of an Ivanoff water-correcting lens to the camera.

The experiments in 1963 were only the first step in our plans to map wrecks stereo-photogrammetrically from a small submarine, although virtually all of the naval, oceanographic and cartographic authorities we consulted advised us that it would be impossible. On 28 May 1964, the *Asherah*, a two-man submarine, was launched by the Electric Boat Division of General Dynamics in Groton, Connecticut [Pl. 38–39]. Ordered by the University of Pennsylvania Museum, financially assisted by the National Geographic Society and the National Science Foundation, it was not only the first submarine ever built for archaeology, but the first non-military submarine ever sold by the Electric Boat Company in its sixty-year history.

The *Asherah*, named after a Phoenician goddess of the sea, was designed to carry a pilot and an observer safely to depths of 600

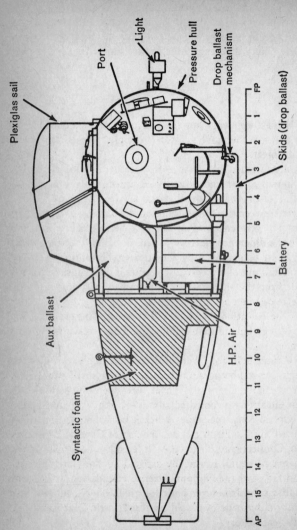

Figure 32. Section of the Asherah

Figure 33. The *Asherah* mapping a Late Roman wreck
photogrammetrically

feet [Fig. 32]. These men sit inside the vessel's pressure hull, a
five-foot sphere pierced with six viewing ports. Surrounding them
are such instruments as indicators for speed, depth, air pressure,
oxygen and carbon dioxide, as well as a voltmeter, gyro-compass,
sub-to-diver communications system, sub-to-surface communications system, rebreathing system, speed-control system, and a
panel of electric switches for interior and exterior lights and
cameras. A ton of electric batteries, mounted along with ballast

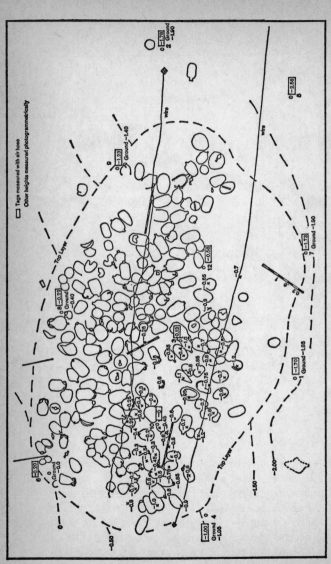

Figure 34. Map of a Late Roman wreck, 140 feet deep, made in a single dive with the *Asherah*. By Rudolf Karius

tanks and compressed-air tanks in the submarine's conical tail, can power the side-mounted motors for up to ten hours. The two motors and propellers are movable, allowing the *Asherah* to go straight up, down, forward or backward, to hover like a helicopter, and to inch its way slowly along the sea-bed. Sixteen feet long and weighing four and a half tons, the vessel moves at speeds up to four knots. On the surface a plexiglass canopy protects its open hatch from breaking waves.

A pair of modified FB-1 aerial survey cameras, encased in watertight housings, were mounted six feet apart on the front of the submarine [Pl. 40]. Specially ground lenses corrected the distortion normally caused by the index of refraction of water. Electric leads into the *Asherah's* pressure hull allowed the co-pilot to take pairs of stereo-photographs at will; the cameras automatically advanced the film after each shot and re-cocked their shutters.

During one dive, the *Asherah* was 'flown' by Yüksel Eğdemir in two passes over a Late Roman wreck lying in 140 feet of water [Fig. 33]. Donald Rosencrantz, acting as co-pilot on the dive, took a series of overlapping pairs of photographs on each pass, completely covering the site. Before an accurate plan with elevations could be made from these pictures, fifty-six hours of laboratory work with the instruments of Holland's International Training Centre for Aerial Survey were needed, but the underwater work had taken less than an hour [Fig. 34]. It would have taken a dozen archaeologists with aqualungs, using the best mapping methods previously devised, many weeks of diving to do the same job.

7. THE TOOLS FOR UNDERWATER EXCAVATION

Following the preliminary mapping of an archaeological site, the actual dissection of the site by excavation begins. Each phase of the digging must, of course, be recorded carefully by methods such as those described in the preceding chapter, for the removal of earth and artifacts destroys the site forever.

The tools of the normal land excavation include picks for breaking the earth, shovels for removing it, and knives and brushes for more delicate digging and cleaning. After the earth has been inspected and even sifted, it is taken away from the excavation area in hand-carried baskets, wheelbarrows, or dump carts on tracks. Sites vary, naturally, and in some rare instances even bulldozers have been used with care, often to the horror of archaeologists not familiar with the special conditions involved.

Of these tools, only the knife can be considered appropriate for underwater excavation, although on small sites covered by only an inch or so of sand, hand-carried buckets have been used as baskets for the removal of the sand. The development of special tools for digging under shallow water and raising objects to the surface began in the nineteenth century, and if these early devices now seem primitive one must remember that only in the last quarter of the nineteenth century were such men as General Pitt Rivers demonstrating the need and means for excavating stratigraphically on land.

It is difficult now to imagine the excitement aroused by the early work on prehistoric Swiss lake dwellings. Sammel Byers, writing in *Harper's New Monthly* of February 1890, noted that 'Tourists will hardly be content any more to pass through Switzerland without visiting one or more of the museums where the collections made from the excavated lake dwellings are exhibited. ... There are hundreds of thousands of specimens of stone, wood, cloth, weapons, and ornaments, of a people whose towns were old a thousand years before grey old excavated Pompeii was ever thought of.'

Our earliest records of the lake dwellings go back to 1472, but it was not until the nineteenth century that their study was begun seriously. Then, during a uniquely dry winter in 1853–54, the levels of many Swiss lakes dropped appreciably. The local farmers, in their efforts to claim some of the newly uncovered land, set to work building retaining walls on the beds of the lakes which they were filling with earth. In the course of this work they came across remains which they reported to the Antiquarian Association of Zürich, then headed by Ferdinand Keller. A dozen years later, Keller described the visit: 'In January 1854, Mr Aeppli of Ober Meilen informed the society at Zürich, that remains of human industry, likely to throw unexpected light on the primaeval history of the inhabitants of the country, had been found near his house in that part of the bed of the lake then left dry by the water.'

Before long the fishermen of the lakes, who often had caught their nets on wooden piles, realized that the remains were not a curse to them. The desire for artifacts, dating from the Stone, Bronze and Iron Ages, grew quickly, and the fishermen began salvaging and selling objects by the thousands. At the same time, more serious excavations were attempted on the sites now being discovered in lakes throughout much of Europe north of the Mediterranean coastal countries. Whilst the work would not meet modern standards, attempts were made to draw stratified sections of the sites, and plans were published.

In some instances the work was conducted on dry land, in areas that had dried naturally and in areas that were being kept dry by constantly running pumps.

'Under ordinary circumstances, however,' wrote Keller in 1890, 'the case is different, and the antiquities have to be looked for in the lake itself, occasionally at considerable depths, either lying on the surface of the lake-bed, or buried to some extent in the mud. In localities where the former case occurs, and where, strange to say, these primaeval antiquities appear still on the surface of the lake bottom after having been exposed for thousands of years to the gaze of every boatman who passed over them, all

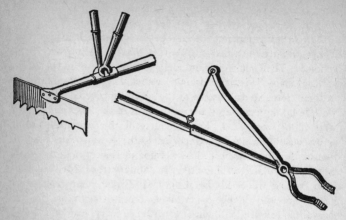

Figure 35. a, scraper and b, forceps (From F. Keller)

that is required is a keen eye, clear still water, and a pair of forceps similar to those represented in the annexed woodcut [Fig. 35b]. This simple instrument is fixed to the end of a long pole, and as will be seen from the sketch opens and shuts by means of a cord.

'But where the antiquities are buried in the mud, the labour is much greater; in this case a kind of implement similar to that drawn in the annexed woodcut, is used for trenching the bottom [Fig. 35a]. The scraper itself is fixed to a strong pole, and is pressed down into the mud by means of two wooden handles attached to it by sockets and rings; these handles are worked from the boat above. This arrangement makes the scraper more effective, so that trenches can be dug, or rather scraped, of a considerable depth, and a large quantity of mud can be collected together, which is then brought up by the usual implements and examined. It is obvious that this operation must be very difficult where the ground is encumbered by stumps of piles or stones; and it is but due to the Swiss antiquaries to mention the difficulties with which they have to contend in pursuing their investigations.'

Obviously, much of the work in the lakes was no more than the salvaging of artifacts, which has been described more fully in another chapter, but the scientific efforts revealed that most Swiss lakes, as well as many of those in the surrounding regions of Italy, Austria, and Hungary, were settled by people who lived in entire villages of wattle-and-daub supported on wooden piles. More than a hundred settlements, some covering acres and resting on thousands of sharpened tree stems, existed in a single lake. The villages had first been founded in the European Neolithic period, but many were inhabited continuously through the Bronze and Iron Ages; some lasted even into Roman times. Whether the villages were supported above water or above only swampy ground poses a problem which cannot be solved until the contemporary levels of the lakes can be determined to the satisfaction of all, but at least we know that some were connected to dry land by bridges resting also on piles; the absence of piles leading to shore in other cases suggests that contact was maintained only by the dug-out canoes which have been raised from some of the lakes.

The work of Colonel Friedrich Schwab should be mentioned here, for it was in looking for lake dwellings and their artifacts that he made a discovery of greatest importance to European archaeology. The prehistoric mound of La Tène, at the east end of Lake Neuchâtel, is partly covered by water. There, from a small area only 3 feet deep, Schwab salvaged an impressive group of spearheads and swords. For three years afterwards, he rowed over the lake on calm days when he could look out from his boat, specially built for viewing, and pick up artifacts with a grab he had devised. The grab gathered in the mud surrounding each artifact, thus protecting the objects themselves. Most of the excavation at La Tène took place on land, following draining operations which began in 1868, but Schwab's original investigations under water had brought to light those pieces which would come to characterize the culture of Western and Central Europe during the second half of the Iron Age, a culture now known as the La Tène civilization.

The crude tools devised for digging into lake bottoms were operated from the surface, but the shallow depths usually allowed the investigators to see what they were doing. How much more difficult it would be to dig successfully in deep water from the surface is obvious, but it has been tried. Two attempts to excavate ships, sunk far apart in time and place, were made with surface-operated grabs before such an approach was abandoned. Both projects should be considered as salvage rather than as true excavation, but because they represent a stage in the development of tools for underwater excavation they are included in this chapter. Neither of the operations would have been attempted had better means been available, but both produced results of value.

Shortly before General Cornwallis' surrender to General Washington at Yorktown in 1781, ending the American War of Independence, a number of British warships were sunk in the York River, both intentionally, to form a blockade against a feared French fleet, and as a result of enemy action. Shortly afterwards, and during the following century, salvage operations were conducted, but broken oystermen's tongs and entangled fishing lines indicated that the wrecks still remained in 1934.

At that time, the Mariners' Museum of Newport News, Virginia, and the Colonial National Historical Park joined forces to drag the river and plot the positions of the sunken ships. Promising sites were inspected by professional divers who saw a number of wrecks, but found them too poorly preserved to be raised or even identified exactly; fortunately, their construction may be studied on original Admiralty drawings. The divers and a clam-shell grab lowered from the surface, however, retrieved an excellent representative collection of typical equipment and armament of the eighteenth century. Among the cannon, anchors, tools, rope, crockery, balance weights, and pewter, was a large number of rum bottles. The condition of the bottles, originally of dark olive-green glass, caused Homer Ferguson, president of the Mariners' Museum, to remark at length on the 'brilliantly variegated scales' which crusted their surfaces. Little did anyone realize the importance of those iridescent layers.

Robert Brill, of the Corning Museum of Glass, discovered that the number of decomposition layers on a glass specimen is directly related to the number of years the glass has been buried or submerged. The exact cause of these 'weathering crusts' is not known, but one layer seems to form each year, probably from changes in temperature or the alternation between dry and rainy seasons. Counting the layers under a microscope, therefore, reveals the length of time a piece of glass has been in soil or water. Brill compares the method to tree-ring counting, 'except that a destructive process is involved rather than a process of growth'.

A bottle from the York River provided one of the best tests of Brill's technique. An average of 156 layers was counted, and if that figure 'is subtracted from 1935, the year in which the piece was excavated, a submersion date of 1779 is obtained, in good agreement with the known date of 1781'. Such specimens, whose date of submersion or burial is known exactly, are rare, but another bottle was provided for a check. This time it was from the underwater operations at Port Royal, which the waters engulfed during the earthquake in 1692 (see p. 85). Various counts gave dates for the onset of weathering as 1685, 1691, and 1701. Underwater archaeology had aided indirectly the development of a new dating technique for all archaeologists.

The second attempt to excavate an ancient vessel with a clamshell grab took place in 1950 at Albenga, Italy, where a wreck of the first century B.C. had been known since 1925 from findings in fishermen's nets. Archaeologist Nino Lamboglia, director of the Institute of Ligurian Studies, after failing to secure either divers or government funds for an excavation of the site, received the offer of *Artiglio II*, a professional salvage ship of great fame. Helmet divers removed a few amphoras, but most of the work was done by a great grab which smashed into the wreck and filled its steel jaws with amphoras, wood, and metal. The grab was directed by an observer in an underwater chamber, connected by telephone with those on the surface, but no attempt to map the remains was made. The expedition was a failure. Lamboglia was the first to admit it, and through his own self-criticism became a leading pioneer in developing methods of making accurate plans of underwater sites. Such methods were to change underwater salvage operations into true archaeology.

Mechanical dredging machines obviously did not provide a method for either raising the objects from a deep site or removing their covering of sand and mud. Divers, on the other hand, could not perform as gangs of workmen, shovelling earth into wheelbarrows or railway wagons as on land. Something new was needed. The 'shovel' of underwater archaeology, namely the air lift, was used first in archaeology by Jacques-Yves Cousteau, the father of modern diving, during his excavation of the Roman wreck at the Grand Congloué island near Marseilles. Since that time it has been used on virtually every major excavation under water.

The air lift is a type of suction hose. It is simply a vertical pipe or tube, of metal, reinforced rubber, or plastic, to whose lower end air is pumped through a hose from a compressor on the surface. As the air enters the tube near its bottom, it rises naturally through the tube towards the surface in the form of bubbles; the bubbles increase in size and speed as they move upward through ever-decreasing pressure. The action causes a suction at the mouth of the tube, pulling in water, as well as mud, sand, and other material small enough to enter it. The air lift can be quite powerful and must be used with care. Except for trenching in areas thought to be devoid of archaeological interest, it is best operated by keeping its mouth a few inches away from the bottom of the sea, while sweeping sand gently toward it by hand. Thus the danger of breaking fragile wood is eliminated, and most small artifacts can be noted and placed aside before they take the potentially dangerous trip up through the pipe. It should also be remembered that the original position of any object air-lifted from a site is lost, even if the object itself is retrieved later.

The air lift can be either tall enough to discharge the water, mud, and broken shells on the surface, or it can discharge under water; in both cases some filtering system is necessary to catch any artifacts which may have entered the tube. The diameter of the tube depends on the job in hand, but usually ranges between 3 and 10 inches.

At Grand Congloué [Fig. 36] the air lift, 4.7 inches in diameter, was at first simply lowered from a ship on the surface, but the divers quickly discovered that wave action affected even the lower end of the pipe. The flexible air-lift pipe was then run out from Grand Congloué island along an 85-foot wooden boom, from which it dropped straight into the water and down to the wreck

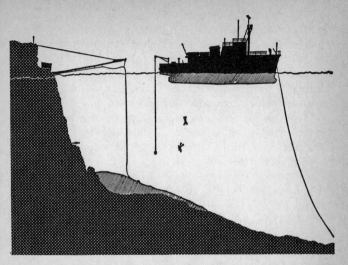

Figure 36. The first use of the air lift for archaeology; Grand Congloué

130 feet below the surface; its upper end emptied into the sea through a filtering basket on the island.

The lesson learned at Grand Congloué, that a rocking ship does not provide a stable support for an air lift, has been learned elsewhere, but in calm water a surface float can be a most suitable support. At submerged Port Royal, where countless cubic yards of mud had to be removed, Edwin Link used a metal air-lift pipe ten inches in diameter [Pl. 42]. As at Grand Congloué, the upper end of the pipe rose above the surface of the water and disgorged into open air, but this time the discharge fell onto a small barge which allowed the water to run off its deck while being inspected for artifacts. Link used the same air lift in Israel during his investigation of the Roman port of Caesarea. A similar system was used during the operation in the sacred well at Chichen Itza (see p. 69); there, the upper end of the tube emerged through a hole in the centre of a raft built specially to catch and filter the mud and water which spouted into the air [Pl. 17].

The crude rakes and hooks used for digging into the beds of Swiss lakes during the nineteenth century have now been replaced by the air lifts. In 1961, divers from the Underwater Sports Centre of Neuchâtel began the scientific excavation of Champréveyres, one of more than a hundred sites under the surface of their lake [Fig. 37]. Under the Centre's president, Willy Haag, they carefully divided the Bronze Age settlement into a hundred squares of 1 metre each with tape. Then, using a flexible pipe of reinforced rubber, about 6 inches in diameter, they air-lifted each area. Bones, sherds, and seeds from each square, after being caught in a sieve floating on the surface of the lake, were kept separate for further study. Remarkably, Haag and his group demonstrated the possibility of excavating stratigraphically under water, and their photographs show the clearly defined strata of the lake bed with its 3,000-year-old habitation layers.

So far we have discussed rather special cases of the use of air lifts: Champréveyres is only 10 feet deep, the well at Chichen Itza is completely calm, Port Royal and Caesarea required the raising of masses of mud not usually encountered, and the island of Grand Congloué provided a solid base not always found near underwater sites. There is probably no better example of equipment adapted to special needs by the underwater archaeologist than the air lift used by Robert Wheeler's group from the Minnesota Historical Society in another special case. In order to follow the early fur-traders' routes, the divers and archaeologists must themselves travel by small boats and must often make overland hikes around the rapids which destroyed so many of the voyageurs' canoes. Wheeler's team, therefore, devised an air lift whose tube, float, and sieve are all made of light aluminium sections which can be broken down and folded together. The entire air lift can be carried easily in a back pack by one man, yet it forms a sturdy, 30 foot-long air lift when reassembled.

On relatively deep sites in the open sea, where there is no near-by land, it is usually best to hang the top of an air lift from underwater buoys rather than from surface floats, and to allow it to empty under water. Thus the tube is never affected by the possible movement of a raft or boat above, even in the roughest weather, and the objects which inadvertently may enter its mouth are not shot violently through the air when they reach its upper end.

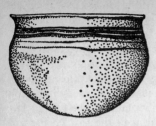

Figure 37. Bronze bracelet and pottery bowl from Champréveyres (after Haag)

During its investigations in 1955 of the Mahdia wreck, from which so many art objects had been salvaged previously by sponge divers, the Underwater Research Club of Tunisia anchored their rigid metal air lift to the sea-bed with two cables; a pair of air-filled floats attached to the upper part of the air-lift tube kept it vertical in the water. The top of the tube was fitted with a filtering basket through which it discharged 80 feet above the wreck site, but still 45 feet below the violent surface movement of the waves. The tube, only 3 inches in diameter, was moved easily around the site by shortening one anchor cable and lengthening the other; additional manoeuvrability was got from a flexible metal section at the lower end of the tube.

Another ship of the Roman Republic, as if it had not suffered enough by running on to a reef near Cape Dramont in France, and sinking in 115 feet of water, was badly robbed by souvenir hunters and then dynamited following its discovery and preliminary examination by Claude Santamaria. Nevertheless, enough remained of the wreck to attract Frederic Dumas and A. Sivirine to the site for further study in 1959. In order to cut a trench through the wreck for a look at its hull construction, the two French divers obtained the flexible but extremely heavy tube used at Grand Congloué. As at Mahdia, the tube was suspended from an underwater float which was anchored to the sea-bed; this time the top of the tube was about 20 feet below the water's surface. Artifacts, such as pieces of pottery, were allowed to spew out of the top of the air lift, but they settled quickly back on to the site while mud and sand drifted away in the current; the divers even considered methods which would have caused the sherds also to fall away from the site, but valuable artifacts might have been lost by such a move.

During its excavation of the Bronze Age shipwreck at Cape Gelidonya, the University of Pennsylvania Museum used two air lifts [Fig. 38]. One, of alternating rigid and flexible sections, was only 3 inches in diameter, but it was long enough to reach the surface where it emptied through a filter on the boat 95 feet above the site; as usual, the movement of the boat on the surface made this a rather inefficient arrangement. Much better was a larger air lift, 6 inches in diameter, which was made of rigid sections of metal tube except for its reinforced rubber lower end [Pl. 43]. Anchored securely to the sea-bed, the tube rose to a point only 45 feet above the wreck, where it was supported by an empty gasoline can. A cloth bag with a very loose mesh was tied over the top of the tube to filter out larger objects such as pieces of pottery, but, although this functioned fairly well, a definite improvement was needed.

The following year, in 1961, when the University Museum began its excavation of the Byzantine wreck at Yassi Ada, diver Claude Duthuit constructed a large wire basket which he bolted to the top of the air-lift pipe [Fig. 39, Pl. 41]. The basket funnelled down into a large cloth bag which was suspended beneath it by four rings. The wire basket allowed almost all of the sand and mud from the wreck to be carried away by the current, but larger pieces, such as pebbles and shells, were caught by the mesh of the wire and fell into the bag; thus very little material rained back down on the site once it had been sucked up through the tube. The bag, when full, was attached to a rope by a diver and hauled to the barge above, where it was emptied out onto the deck and thoroughly searched by hand. A number of coins and important bits of pottery were saved from loss in this manner, and even a fragile glass medallion took the trip through the tube without suffering the slightest damage.

It has been mentioned that the air lift should not be used for direct excavation into an ancient wreck, although at Grand Congloué a short length of pipe of small diameter was attached

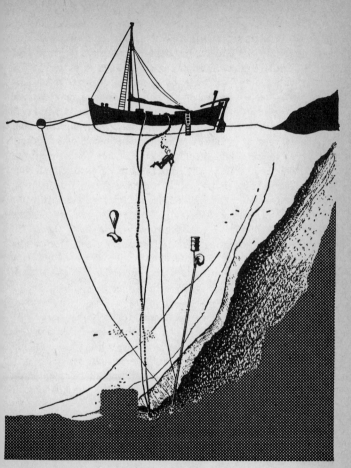

Figure 38. The air lifts used at Cape Gelidonya

to the mouth of the air lift, reducing the size of the nozzle and allowing careful work among pieces of pottery in the ancient cargo. For the future, Frederic Dumas has suggested a most sensible approach to excavation. He recommends cutting a large trench completely around a site with a big and powerful air lift. Sand from the wreck can be swept into this trench, which can be emptied from time to time by the air lift without great concern for sucking up and breaking objects in it. Actual excavation is done by hand : the underwater archaeologist quickly learns that he can cut the mud away from a piece of wood or pottery, without moving the artifact itself, by means of currents formed by short, well-directed strokes of his hand; this mud may then be raised into the water, again by hand, to form clouds which are removed easily with broad, sweeping movements of the arms and hands. In some instances, especially where roots of sea growth make such digging difficult, large blocks of mud may be cut out with a knife and carried away from the site; or metal claws, such as those used at Spargi and later at Cape Gelidonya, may be used.

Commandant Philippe Tailliez, in an amazing demonstration of the careful work which can be done by non-professional archaeologists, laid down exacting rules for the use of the air lift in 1957. While excavating the mid-first century B.C. Titan wreck at Ile du Levant, near Toulon [Pl. 44], he instructed his navy divers that any interesting artifact uncovered by the air lift should be left *in situ* and its position plotted; even then it could not be moved without the advice of the excavation supervisor. During this well-disciplined operation, the navy divers even became quite expert at sorting and mending the bits of broken pottery which arrived at their surface vessel through the air lift. It is worth noting that Tailliez in France and, later, Haag in Switzerland, both of whose projects stand out as shining examples of amateur archaeology, ended their excavation reports bemoaning the lack of archaeologists on their staffs.

All of these Mediterranean wrecks on which air lifts were used, with the exceptions of the wrecks at Cape Gelidonya and Yassi Ada, were of merchant ships which sank during the final two centuries of the pre-Christian era. With the same exceptions, for one reason or another, none of these ships was ever fully excavated. In four cases sections of keels were either raised to the surface or drawn, but in no instance were plans of the edge-joined hull planking made far from the keel. Nevertheless, Grand

Figure 39. Yassi Ada; the air-lift anchor ropes were later moved farther up the tube to provide greater movement of the tube

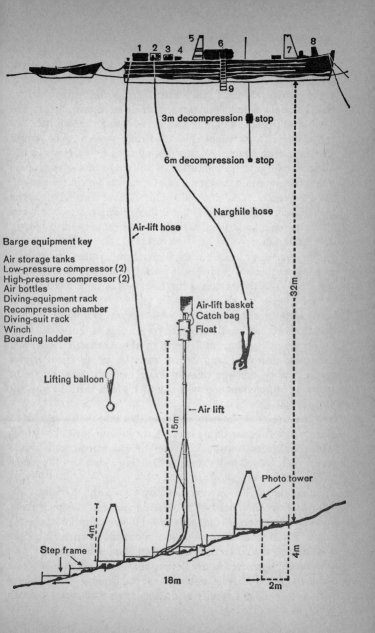

3m decompression stop

6m decompression stop

Narghile hose

Air-lift hose

Barge equipment key

Air storage tanks
Low-pressure compressor (2)
High-pressure compressor (2)
Air bottles
Diving-equipment rack
Recompression chamber
Diving-suit rack
Winch
Boarding ladder

Air-lift basket
Catch bag
Float

Lifting balloon

← Air lift

15m

32m

Photo tower

Step frame

4m

4m

18m

2m

Congloué, Mahdia, Titan (Ile du Levant), Cape Darmont, and Spargi all provided sites for the development of excavation techniques which are used still today. Further, the early work at Grand Congloué and Titan gave for their time, according to Fernand Benoît, 'the first evidence which we have for the construction and lading of a merchant ship. ... Before this, the only records consisted of illustrations (bas-reliefs, mosaics, frescoes) which had no scale and gave no indication of the shape of the ship's hull below the waterline, and some rare literary and epigraphic texts'. The later work at Mahdia, and F. Dumas' investigation of several wrecks, added to our knowledge of Roman ship construction, and all of the sites yielded valuable hoards of contemporary pottery and other finds.

The reverse of the air lift, the high-pressure water jet, may also be used for removing sand and mud. To prevent its hose from recoiling violently, as does a fire hose, it should be fitted with a special nozzle which sends small jets of water backwards to equalize the reaction from the main stream. The water jet stirs up clouds of mud and endangers fragile objects, but it is useful in certain cases: the deck-house of the American Civil War *Cairo* was cleared of sand with a water jet before it was hauled to the surface, and the tunnels under the *Vasa* were dug with water jets in conjunction with air lifts which carried away the loosened mud.

If the stream of water is sent through a pipe with a hole in its side, mud will be sucked up through the hole and into the stream, which will carry it away from the immediate area, perhaps to a sieve. Such a device was used by Donald P. Jewell on inundated Indian mounds in California.

Either the air lift or water jet may be used for probing a site with trial trenches, but two prospecting tools can also be of assistance. Core samplers [Pl. 46] may reveal the stratification of various parts of a site, but because of their potential damage to unique objects they should be used only when absolutely necessary, and then with great care. A safe device, but one which cannot locate wood and pottery, is the underwater metal detector; this has been used with excellent results in finding deposits of metal beneath mud and sand [Pl. 45].

There is, however, sometimes more than sand and mud to be removed. Coralline concretion, hard as cement, often covers wrecks or parts of their cargoes. On the ancient shipwreck at Cape Gelidonya this concretion was up to eight inches thick, and its removal was the major problem in the excavation of that unique site.

After the exciting discovery of this Bronze Age shipwreck off the southwest coast of Turkey, Peter Throckmorton wrote to John Huston of the Council of Underwater Archaeology in San Francisco. One of the purposes of the Council was to acquaint divers and archaeologists with one another, and in this case Throckmorton was advised to contact the University of Pennsylvania Museum, which already was working on land in Turkey. Before long the Museum's first underwater expedition was formed, with Throckmorton as technical adviser, Frederic Dumas as chief diver, and Joan du Plat Taylor, with support from the London University Institute of Archaeology, in charge of conserving and recording the finds; I was sent to the local Y.M.C.A. to learn to dive.

After pitching camp on a narrow beach a few miles from the site, we began to sail out each day, in local sponge boats, to the the island against which the ancient ship must have run. There we dived twice a day to the wreck 90–5 feet below. Almost everything was invisible beneath the rock-hard concretion, but here and there the corners and ends of a few metal objects protruded. These showed that the ship had settled partially between the base of the island and a huge boulder; the first of a number of photographic montages was made of the site by a free diver, and positions of visible artifacts were plotted on sheets of frosted plastic.

With each of the eight divers working little more than an hour a day on the site, it would have been impossible to extract from the concretion each tiny artifact, including bits of pottery and thin fragments of metal, without hopelessly breaking them. Dumas wisely suggested raising the entire cargo in still concreted masses which could later be rejoined like the pieces of a giant jig-saw puzzle; the raised 'site' could then be excavated on land at our small camp. Thus pertinent points on various masses were plotted, and then divers with hammers and chisels spent weeks cutting these massive lumps free from the sea-bed, a task that was greatly hampered by the strong current which forced excavators to hold to rocks with their legs to avoid being swept away while working. An underwater pneumatic hammer would be a great addition to a similar project in the future.

The first large mass of encrusted cargo was deeply circumscribed, but it refused to budge from the sea-bed. Throckmorton and Dumas brought the hydraulic jack from the expedition jeep and placed it under the lump. The 300-pound lump was jacked up until it broke free of the sea-bed, and then it was winched to the sponge boat above. By using this seemingly violent method, not one artifact was broken while being raised; surely most would have suffered badly had we attempted to extricate them separately under water.

Once reassembled on the beach, the lumps were again photographed, and the concretion was then removed with an assortment of hammers and chisels, including an electric vibrating point [Pl. 50]. It was also found that the concretion shattered and fell cleanly away from solid metal following repeated careful taps with a hammer. The cleaned objects, still holding their original relationships to one another, were next drawn in detail and added to the master plan of the site which up to this time had shown only vague masses.

The ship had settled, unfortunately, onto a bare, rocky bottom, with far too little sand to cover and preserve its wooden hull. It was with some excitement, therefore, that we saw fragments of wood protruding from beneath a large mass of concretion at one end of the site. At the same time, the wood presented a problem that was solved only with another tool of underwater archaeology which is now standard on any underwater dig. We feared that if we tried to raise the concretion with the winch from the surface, the slightest roll of the boat would allow the heavy mass to smash the wood beyond repair. Dumas, however, had brought two balloons of plastic cloth which were capable of lifting 400 pounds apiece. As each piece of concretion was chiselled from above the wood, a deflated balloon was tied to it and filled with air from a hose or aqualung; the lumps then floated safely and easily to the surface [Pl. 49]. Finally, after divers had spent weeks cutting through the solid rock on which it rested, the wood itself was ballooned to the surface in one mass exactly as it had rested on the sea-bed. Only at this time were the lead-shoed and helmeted sponge divers used, for with their heavy outfits each could swing a sledge hammer on to a chisel held by a scuba diver.

The wood was most fragmentary, but it did includes pieces of planks with tree-nails fitted into bored holes, just as in Homer's description of the ship built by Odysseus. The interior of the hull was lined with brushwood dunnage, the bark still well preserved, which finally explained the purpose of the brushwood used by Odysseus, a point which has caused Classicists trouble in translation and interpretation [Pl. 51].

At the conclusion of the excavation we had the picture of a small sailing vessel, about 35 feet long according to the distributions of finds, which carried more than a ton of metal cargo. By carefully plotting the position of each object in the wreck, we were later able to determine that all of the personal items on board came from an area at one end of the ship; these included a cylinder seal for stamping official documents, five scarabs, the merchant's balance-pan weights, traces of food (olive stones and possible bird and fish bones), a pair of stone maceheads, a crescent-bladed razor, chunks of crystal, whetstones for sharpening tools, and the single oil lamp on board. The area, it is assumed, was the cabin or some sort of living quarters, and these objects surely belonged to the captain or crew. A sheep's knuckle bone in this 'cabin area' could have been used either to while away the hours playing the common game of knuckle bones, or it could have been for the purpose of divination, often used by ancient mariners to guide them on their way.

The results of the Cape Gelidonya excavation were both spectacular and of great historical importance. The metal cargo formed by far the largest hoard of pre-Classical copper and bronze implements ever found in the Aegean area. It consisted largely of four-handled copper ingots, weighing about 55 pounds apiece and often stamped with signs in the still undeciphered Cypro-Minoan script. These ingots, as well as smaller disc-shaped ingots of bronze, were neatly stacked in the ship and held together with

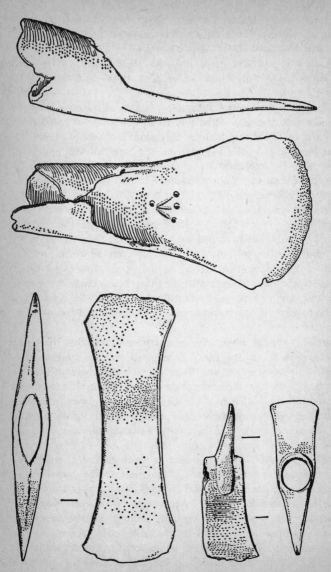

Figure 40. Bronze implements from Cape Gelidonya, by Terry Ball

mat wrappings. Bronze implements included hoes, picks, axes, adzes, a shovel, chisels, knives, bowls, pins, spearheads, and a spit; most had been broken in antiquity and had been packed into wicker baskets along with pieces of broken ingots [Fig. 40, Pl. 48]. On board too were many pieces of casting waste, as well as tools which had been cast, but never hammered or sharpened. The cargo, then, was a load of scrap metal, destined to be melted down and cast into new weapons or tools. The ship also carried the two necessary ingredients for making new bronze: the copper ingots and ingots of tin, the earliest ever found.

Could the merchantman have carried a tinker on board? A bronze swage block, for drawing out pins and hammering sockets on tools, was found, along with the stone mace-heads or hammers with the very smooth surfaces necessary for hammering out sheets of metal. A large stone, weighing 160 pounds and thus far larger than any of the fist-sized ballast stones found on the site, was resting on plank fragments near the middle of the ship; a rather flat side of the hard, close-grained stone suggests that it was used as an anvil at a time, before the use of iron, when anvils were only of stone. Perhaps the most striking indication of metal-working on the ship came from the whetstones and polishers found in the 'cabin' area.

A study of the pottery by Miss Taylor and J. B. Hennessy revealed that most of it dated to a period within fifty years of 1200 B.C., and an independent dating of some of the brushwood by the radiocarbon method gave exactly the same range. A determination of the nationality and route of the ship, which sailed while Homer's heroes may have been alive, became most important. The cargo of copper ingots and bronze tools was almost completely identifiable as Cypriot, but the ship itself was not necessarily from Cyprus.

First, an analysis of the stone balance-pan weights revealed that they formed several sets which were far more accurate than had been believed possible by archaeologists, who seldom find contemporary weights so well grouped in land excavations. The sets proved that the ship could have traded with Egypt, Syria, Palestine, Cyprus, Troy, the Hittite Empire, Crete, and probably the Greek mainland. This told us little about the route of the ship, but added precious information about trade 3,000 years ago.

The careful plotting of every object on the wreck had allowed us to judge which were personal possessions and which were only items of trade in the hold. From this came the clue to the ship's origin. The one piece of pottery on board which could have been considered part of the ship's equipment, rather than a vessel for cargo such as wine or oil, was the lamp, and it was Syro-Palestinian in type. The mace-heads and two stone mortars on board seem also to be Syrian. The scarabs were not Egyptian, as originally suspected, but Syro-Palestinian copies of Egyptian scarabs. The cylinder seal, of the kind every Near Eastern merchant used, was Syrian. The suggestion that all of these things were merely trinkets picked up as souvenirs by Mycenaean Greek sailors must be abandoned; in that case, would there not have been at least one Greek item in the cabin?

Everything pointed to the Bronze Age ship having sailed from Syria to Cyprus, where it took on a cargo of scrap metal before its last tragic trip westward, but it seemed impossible. Syrian or Canaanite or Phoenician sailors were not, according to most authorities, supposed to have begun their famous sea trade as early as 1200 B.C.; indeed, one of the main reasons for dating Homer so much later than the events about which he wrote is his frequent mention of Phoenician merchants. The real excitement of the excavation, therefore, took place far away from Cape Gelidonya, in dry museums and libraries.

A careful study of four-handled copper ingots in Egyptian tomb-paintings revealed that they were not, as is usually believed, depicted most often as tribute from the Aegean, but almost always from Syria; it is further noteworthy that such ingots are excavated on land most often on Sardinia and Cyprus, two islands later colonized by Phoenicians. Then a re-examination of the bronze implements from Gelidonya showed that most of their prototypes were to be found in Syria and Palestine earlier than in Greece. This seemed to be an even stronger indication that Canaanite or Phoenician merchants were responsible for the cargo and the ship, and since there was no indication whatsoever that the ship was Greek or Cypriot, we must conclude that Phoenician sailors roamed the Mediterranean at the time of Odysseus. Homer's picture of the Bronze Age was made still more convincing by another archaeological excavation. And this excavation had brought together on the sea-bed, for the first time, archaeologists and divers for what the experienced Dumas has called the 'first methodical excavation carried to completion'.

8. COMPLETE EXCAVATION

METHODS of diving, searching, mapping, excavating, and conserving are brought together in what must be considered the major task of any field archaeologist, on land or under water: the scientific excavation of a site. Yet as late as 1962, Frederic Dumas, who had dived and worked on numerous wrecks in the Mediterranean, including those at Grand Congloué, Cape Dramont, and Cape Gelidonya, could accurately write: 'Many misleading accounts of "submarine excavations" have appeared in the press but the fact remains that, as yet, no antique wreck has been examined and recorded in its entirety.' This lack no longer exists.

In 1961 the University of Pennsylvania Museum, now assisted by the National Geographic Society, turned from the rather atypical site at Cape Gelidonya, where little more than cargo had been preserved, to another of the many wrecks charted by Peter Throckmorton off the coast of Turkey. It was a Byzantine wreck which had gone onto the dangerous reef at Yassi Island.

With this wreck lying in 120 feet of water, it was immediately evident that we needed both a larger staff than at Cape Gelidonya, and a diving platform larger than a sponge boat. A staff of 15 specialists, many of whom had not dived before, gathered in Bodrum, therefore, where an 80-ton flat barge was obtained and towed out to Yassi Island 16 miles away. The barge was anchored from three points so that its position could be changed during shifting currents to remain always just above the site, and there it rode out the summer, only partially protected against the hard north wind by the low, nearly flat island. We declined to live on the island because of the hundreds of rats which had chased Throckmorton and Mustafa Kapkin away from their first camp three years before; but by the end of the summer rats had somehow reached the barge 100 yards at sea, and at least one man was bitten during his sleep.

Even with our larger staff, the limited time that is practical for work in 120 feet of water necessitated the use of mechanical aids for mapping the site, so the frame devised by Dumas the previous year was placed over the area that seemed, from the scattered terra-cotta roof tiles, to have been the cabin. Plane tables were constructed locally and placed on either side of the wreck for over-all measurements.

The excavators' first task was to clean the wreck of seaweed with wire scrubbing brushes so that the cargo would be clear for photographs and drawings. Then every visible object was labelled with a numbered plastic tag so that it could be identified in the photographs and drawings; stiff wire stems held the tags always facing upwards.

Diving in teams of two or three, the staff began to plot the positions of the objects in the cargo, as well as of the terra-cotta roof tiles. The mapping frame was used, but when it proved quite time-consuming a number of wire grids, both 2 and 3 metres square, were laid over various parts of the wreck [Fig. 41]. Artists with gridded sheets of plastic and graphite pencils hovered over these grids, keeping constantly just above whatever they might be drawing, and always noting the numbers of objects from the identification tags [Pl. 52]. Elevations were taken down from the grid wires, and then elevations on the four corners of the grid were taken either with a plane table or with the mapping frame [Pl. 53]; in order to conserve bottom time, there had been no attempt to level the grids, and the calculation of true elevations later on land added a heavy burden to the architect.

Once objects had been plotted by one of the several means available, the numbers of those objects were made into lists which were carried to the wreck by divers who began the removal of the upper layer of cargo. About 100 of the 900 globular amphoras in the cargo were raised to the surface, often by being filled with air so that they rose like balloons; the other amphoras, nearly identical, were merely set to one side of the site, where they will lie well protected until they may be wanted in some museum. Each amphora was, of course, inspected for any peculiarity before it was checked from the list.

Once an area had been plotted accurately and its material

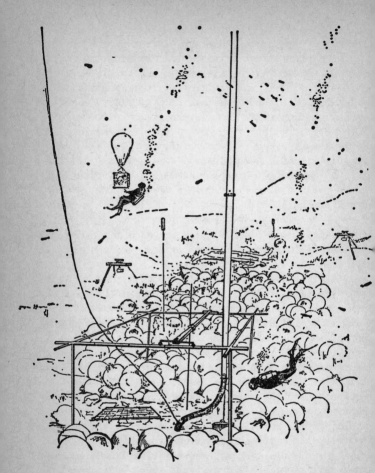

Figure 41. Methods used during first season of excavation at Yassi Ada : mapping frame, plane tables, wire grid, air lift, lifting balloon and basket

removed, a bare expanse of sand often remained above the next level of cargo. It was at this time that the air lift was put into position, its anchor ropes attached far up the tube so that the tube could be swung over an area covering perhaps a third of the wreck without necessitating moving the anchors or changing the lengths of the ropes.

When divers were not diving they were constantly busy. As soon as pottery came to the surface, the thickest sea concretion was mechanically removed with small picks and chisels before it hardened; final cleaning took place later in a bath of dilute hydrochloric acid at the expedition headquarters in Bodrum. Other divers searched for hours through the piles of muck, mostly sand and broken shells, which sometimes came up more than once a day from the air lift. Still others kept time for the excavators below and signalled the ends of dives by hammering on a short length of pipe hung over the side of the barge; the banging could be heard easily on the site. Other divers jumped into the water to retrieve amphoras which popped to the surface like little balloons, and the lifting balloon itself had to be brought to the barge. Below the balloon hung a large wire basket, into which objects of solid material were placed for a speedy trip to the surface; once on the surface, the basket had to be emptied carefully by divers with snorkels. And, when we dived with hookah, every diver had to take his turn tending hose [Pl. 54].

The architect, meanwhile, was transferring the drawn and photographed grids to his master plan of the site.

The two-hour trip to the island and then back every day, as well as the diving, became routine; two or three divers remained always on the barge at night as guards. As director it was often necessary for me to be away from the site on business, and the day to day direction of the digging fell to Frederick van Doorninck, another graduate student of Classical archaeology at the University of Pennsylvania; David Owen, a student at Brandeis University, was often in charge of the diving operations. It came as a rude shock in this routine when Laurence Joline, a biology teacher and our licensed diving instructor, became a sudden victim of 'the bends' and was paralysed from the waist down. Having foolishly believed the advice of a noted diving authority that we would not suffer serious cases of 'the bends' if we over-decompressed, we were unprepared for such an event and it was a number of hours before Joline could be placed in a small, collapsible chamber in Bodrum. The chamber was not made to withstand

the pressures needed for treating such a serious case of 'the bends'
and when Joline came out of the chamber eight hours later hi
condition was not improved. Meanwhile the American consulat
in Izmir had been alerted, and a light Army plane was ready t
take the stricken diver to the large Navy chamber in Istanbul
A flight path had been charted to keep the plane close over th
sea at all times, for if it had crossed high mountains, the adde
drop in pressure in the unpressurized cabin would surely hav
caused a worsening of Joline's condition. After 38 hours in th
Istanbul chamber, followed by a period of hospitalization, he wa
back at the site, but a weakness has remained in one leg sinc
that time. The dive in question had been timed perfectly, wit
extra decompression, and the cause of the trouble has never bee
adequately explained; it was the only affliction suffered in we
over 5,000 dives from the barge.

By the end of the first season, a plan of the visible cargo ha
been made [Fig. 45] which showed six large iron anchors nea
what we thought was the bow of the ship, with a seventh to on
side. The cabin area was itself excavated, and the tiles brought t
the surface. Under and around the tiles were the personal posses
sions of the captain and his crew, and just behind the cabin wa
found the ship's large, wide-mouthed water jar, much like thos
used on Aegean boats today.

Perhaps the most important finds from the cabin were the coins
which totalled 16 of gold and over 40 of copper by the end of th
excavation three years later; these dated the wreck with som
precision. Almost all of the coins depicted the Emperor Heracliu
who ruled between A.D. 610 and 641. Although a complete stud
of the coins has not yet been made, the pottery and other artifact
on the ship seem well placed in the first half of the sevent
century, and most probably about 620.

The pottery from the cabin thus proved to be certainly th
largest dated hoard of Byzantine ware ever found. Plates, cup
bowls, pitchers, and cooking pots in a wide variety of forms cam
to light, along with 20 terra-cotta oil lamps [Fig. 42]. The lamp
alone indicate the value of the excavation, for although simila
lamps are known by the hundreds on land, they have been date
often to the fifth and sixth centuries; now we may be certain tha

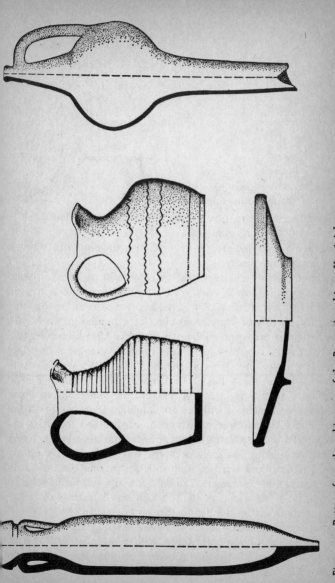

Figure 42. Pottery from the cabin area of the Byzantine ship at Yassi Ada

Figure 43. Censer from the cabin of the Byzantine ship

they are seventh-century types, and if some are found in a destruction level of some land site, the excavator of that site is unlikely to date incorrectly the level and, therefore, the time of the destruction [Pl. 57].

Other finds also appeared in the cabin area. A bronze censer and cross will throw interesting light on the religious practices on board a ship of its time [Fig. 43]. The mercantile interests of the merchantmen were represented also, for a number of steelyards for weighing cargo appeared, one with a lead-filled bronze bust of Athena as its counterweight; since the wine amphoras show no standard of volume, it seems possible that liquids were sold by weight, as are many liquids in Turkey today. For lighter merchandise, there was a set of silver-inlaid bronze balance-pan weights, each marked with its denomination from one pound to one ounce, which was carried in a wooden tray carved with receptacles to fit each weight. Other finds from the cabin included a copper cooking cauldron, a copper tray with a raised rim, a stone mortar, and a pot of resin used for coating the insides of terra-cotta wine containers. The only sure signs of food on board were neat stacks of mussel shells, which may later provide a clue to the route of the ship; a number of animal bones on the site seemed to have been dropped in recent times. Lastly, we learned that members of the crew fished with a wide variety of lead weights, exactly like those used in the Bosphorus today according to our Turkish commissioner, Yüksel Eğdemir.

A few of the ancient crew became known to us as we worked. The captain of the ship had punched in Greek letters at one end of the largest steelyard: George Senior Sea Captain. A glass medallion bore the cruciform monogram of Theodore, and a lead seal bore a similar monogram of the name John – both, of course, in Greek.

As the excavators reached the first signs of the wooden hull, we realized that a more sophisticated method of mapping was needed. It was then that we devised the step-frames and photo-towers described in Chapter 6 [Pl. 54, Fig. 44]. We found, however, when we began to uncover the wood for mapping, that the fragments drifted away in the current, or were displaced by the slightest movements of divers; all of the iron nails which originally held the hull together had rusted away long ago. Improvisation, the secret of all success in the field, provided a solution to the problem. We purchased nearly 2,000 bicycle spokes, and sharpened one end of each. The spokes were pushed through every piece of wood, no matter how tiny, pinning the entire wreck together and to the sea-bed until it could be completely uncovered, examined, and mapped. Divers at that time began to dive without their fins, not really a safe practice, and wearing extra lead so that they could walk easily on the angle-iron of the step-frames without touching the wood.

At the end of the second season, a great deal of wood had been exposed. Fearing that it might be swept away by currents during the winter, we covered the entire site with rubberized cloth from old air mattresses, placed stones on top to hold it in place, and covered this with sand. Curious sponge divers visited the site a number of times before we returned, but they were most careful not to disturb anything.

During the third season we began our experiments with photogrammetric mapping on the last stages of the wreck to be uncovered [Fig. 31]. Excavation went slowly, especially after it was discovered that the wreck extended far up under the sandy slope on which it had come to rest. A deep trench was cut through the silt, therefore, to expose the remains below; the trench was still there the following year, in spite of fairly regular currents, disproving the frequent statement that trenching in underwater

Figure 44. Methods used during second season of excavation at Yassi Ada

archaeology is impossible. In the trench were found four more anchors, making a total of 11, not an unusually large number in antiquity, even for relatively small vessels.

By this time we had established a camp on Yassi Ada, with screened areas for protection against the rats. A schedule was developed so that the architect could swim or row out to the barge, make his dive, and then return to his drawing-board. In the same manner, the photographer, the stereo-specialist, and the artist could all work on the island for most of each day. The

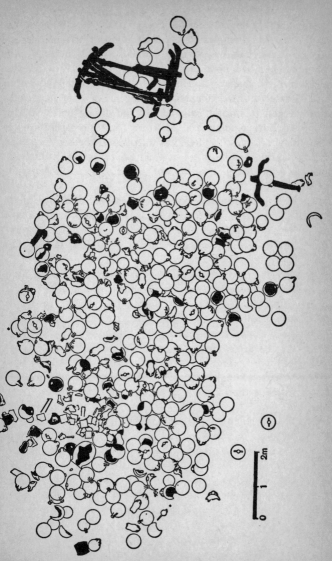

Figure 45. Map of visible layer of cargo on the Byzantine shipwreck at Yassi Ada, by W. Wiener

doctor and the archaeologist-in-charge remained always on the barge, however, along with a sufficient number of divers to handle any emergency; we had obtained by now a sturdy recompression chamber, but had no occasion to use it. Each day a different member of the staff was appointed barge chief. His job was to fuel and operate all of the compressors and generators, to watch pressure gauges, to inspect barge cables and diving hoses, to alert teams of hose tenders, and to insure that the operation ran smoothly and on schedule. Thus all divers, whether they were archaeologists, architects, or photographers, became completely familiar with all aspects of the work, creating a greater margin of safety.

There was a constant effort to increase the efficiency of the work. We preferred diving with 'hookah' hoses, but had only two hoses which would reach from the barge to the wreck. As each pair of divers had to decompress for 21 minutes at the end of a dive, 21 minutes was wasted while the next team waited for the hoses. Therefore, we ran short hoses from air tanks on the barge to the decompression stop so that the divers could change to this air supply while decompressing, thereby releasing the long hoses to be pulled up and used by the waiting team. An underwater 'telephone', simply a piece of string connecting a clipboard and pencil on the decompression stop to a camel bell on the barge, allowed the decompressing divers to inform the next team what had just been accomplished on the site. By such simple methods it was possible almost to double the amount of work done in any one day.

Since the first year of the excavation, every piece of concretion seen on the site had been brought to the surface [Pl. 55]. Georges Barnier and others, working on earlier wrecks, had demonstrated that as iron rusts away on the sea-bed a concretion of sand and shells builds up over it to form a natural mould of the original iron objects; this mould could be cut in half, the mushy iron oxide washed out, and a plaster cast made. Even though we did not know what any particular piece of concretion might be, whether weapon or tool or nail, each was labelled along with the objects in the wreck, and its position was plotted before it was raised to the surface. A backlog of 150 pieces of concretion built up in the Bodrum storeroom while we searched for better methods of casting than those previously used.

An electric lapidary saw, with diamond-edged rotary blade, was obtained to save countless arduous hours of sawing through the rock-hard concretions [Pl. 56]. Naturally, concretion corresponding to the thickness of the saw blade was lost in each cutting, but this was replaced by carefully cut cardboard shims for absolute accuracy in the finished casts. At the same time, various synthetic rubber compounds were tested for a casting material, and that finally selected by Joline and van Doorninck proved far superior to brittle, white plaster; not only was the rubber compound pliable yet firm, but a thin layer of iron oxide from each mould adhered to it, giving the finished casts the realistic appearance of original, but slightly rusty, iron implements.

Our seemingly blind habit of plotting and collecting every scrap of any material on the site produced excellent results in the case of the nondescript concretions. Michael Katzev, another graduate student who learned to dive for archaeology, cast most of the iron, and his study of the pieces has revealed double-headed axes, pickaxes, a hoe, a shovel, a set of bill-hooks, and a pruning hook [Fig. 46]. 'Such implements,' reports Katzev, 'vividly illustrate the independent nature of Byzantine merchant ships, capable of landing at well protected coves to replenish their firewood or cut timber to refit some part of the ship damaged in storm.' Katzev also brought to light an adze, a claw hammer, hammers for metal working, knives, brace-bits, wood gouges, punches, files, dividers, chisels, and sacks of nails for carpentry repairs, as well as a set of barnacle scrapers and an iron caulking knife, all of which further indicated the self-sufficiency of the seventh-century vessel.

The wood of the ship was raised last from the site, but normal lifting methods could not be used on such fragile material. For this job a wire basket 18 feet long and capable of holding the largest preserved timbers, was built with a number of handles on its sides. Divers lowered the basket from the barge to the sea-bed, gently placed wood into it, and then, sometimes wearing tennis shoes, walked with the basket up the slope toward the island 100 yards away and 120 feet above [Pl. 59].

Except when it was being examined, the raised wood was kept

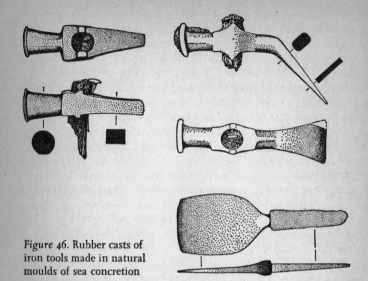

Figure 46. Rubber casts of iron tools made in natural moulds of sea concretion

in basins of water, where it will remain until it can be treated chemically. Waterlogged wood shrinks, cracks, and warps out of all recognition when allowed to dry quickly, unless some substance replaces the water as it evaporates from the cells of the wood. The most successful preservative to date seems to be polyethylene glycol (PEG) which, when dissolved in water, soaks into the wood cells and remains as the water vanishes. The *Vasa* is being conserved with PEG, Robert Inverarity has used it with great success on his colonial bateaux from Lake George, and wooden pieces from Spanish galleons, so soft that they may be easily crushed by hand, are being restored to perfect condition by Alan Albright using carefully controlled techniques in the Smithsonian Institution laboratories.

The excavation and study of the Byzantine hull was left completely to Frederick van Doorninck, who has brilliantly reconstructed much of it from keel to deck beams. He found that most of the hull was constructed in the normal Graeco-Roman manner, with the shell built first, of planks joined at their edges with tenons, and the ribs added later. The upper part of the hull,

owever, was certainly built in the modern manner, with the
keleton of frames put into place first and then covered with
rakes or hull planks. Thus the Byzantine ship may show, for
he first time, the transition between ancient and modern methods
f building wooden ships.

This reconstruction might seem to indicate that the Yassi Ada
hip was simply well preserved, but in fact that was not the case.
: was no better preserved than some other ships which have been
ound on the sea-bed, but with unbelievable patience van Door-
inck was able to piece together its hundreds of tiny clues. Even
fter the wood had been excavated thoroughly, I think that none
f us on the staff thought that he would be able to determine
uch from the mangled scraps of wood.

The bow of the ship had been held above the protective silt by
ocks, so only the stern half of the hull was preserved at all. Even
ere, van Doorninck noted, the areas of well-preserved planking
vere not large, and 'surviving sections of the ribs are so few, so
ttentuated in length, and so widely scattered that they practi-
ally escape our notice at first glance.' He was able to reconstruct
o much of the hull only because 'we now have nearing completion
n the drawing board an accurate state plan of every surviving
crap of wood of a size of any consequence found within this area
omplete with every nail hole, bolt hole, score-line, mortise, or
ny other significant feature.'

In order to do this, each fragment of wood had been labelled
nd photographed in place on the sea-bed, and the labels kept on
ne wood when it came to the surface [Pls. 58, 60, 61]. There,
sing the underwater photographs and labels as guides, van
Doorninck pieced each plank back together for detailed drawings.

Further, from the careful plotting of every object in the cargo
nd in the cabin area, it was possible for van Doorninck to
etermine almost exactly the line of the forward wall of the now
issing wooden cabin. The cabin sat well back towards the stern
f the ship, its floor one-fourth covered, probably on the port side,
y a hearth of flat tiles. This hearth rested in a bed of clay
upported by iron bars, which would not have been known if the
ositions of the concretions, which revealed the bars only as
ubber casts, had not been carefully noted.

Careful excavation provided still more evidence about th
vanished cabin. Although certain 'luxury class' ships are know
to have had tiled roofs, no existing representation of an ordinar
Roman merchant ship shows a cabin with roof tiles. From th
accurate plans of the distribution of tiles at Yassi Ada, however
van Doorninck could be quite certain that the tiles 'were eithe
directly over the cabin or in the cabin when the ship sank. O
these two alternatives, the number of roof tiles, their size an
their proportional distribution into various types clearly favour
the former.' Similar tiles had been found on almost every Roman
ship previously studied in the Mediterranean, but in no case wer
their original positions carefully noted, and there had been som
controversy over their real function.

We have been asked if it was really necessary to label ever
object and to map within several centimetres the positions o
hundreds of wine jars in the cargo. Perhaps the exact placemen
of jars in the middle of the wreck was unimportant, but ther
was no way of knowing this during the excavation. Not only th
position and size of its cabin, but even the length of the 70-foo
merchantman were learned from the distribution of cargo; an
only by experimentation on the less sensitive parts of the wrec
had we developed the means to map accurately the wood when i
was found.

Besides its unique hoards of pottery, iron tools, and miscel
laneous finds, van Doorninck writes, Yassi Ada 'will make severa
important contributions to the history of naval architecture. Thi
would not have been the case if the excavation had been only par
tial, or if the principles of land excavation had not been applied.

But this was only a beginning. Since 1964 three more wreck
in the Mediterranean have been excavated in their entirety : a
late second-century Roman ship carrying a cargo of sarcophag
was excavated by Peter Throckmorton in Italy near Taranto
Michael and Susan Womer Katzev went on from Yassi Ada t
excavate a fourth-century B.C. merchantman off Kyrenia, Cyprus
and I returned to Yassi Ada for the fourth-century A.D. amphor
carrier which we had earlier mapped with the *Asherah*. All wer
University of Pennsylvania Museum projects, the last two jointl
sponsored by the National Geographic Society.

The first order of business in planning for the new excavation at Yassi Ada was to find the means for increasing efficiency. A study of the diving logs from our excavation of the Byzantine ship revealed that we had spent 1,244 hours on that wreck in 3,533 individual dives. Simple arithmetic shows that had the ship been on land, it could have been excavated in one month by only five men working eight-hour days; yet we had worked for four summers, usually with a dozen to fifteen men.

Further, we learned from the logs how we had spent our time: 204 hours (19 per cent of the total) making plans under water, 115 hours (11 per cent) raising cargo and ballast, 41 hours (4 per cent) bringing up the hull remains, and a staggering 693 hours (or 64 per cent of all our time) removing sand from the wreck.

It was clear that on any new project we could greatly lessen the costs of transportation, insurance, rental of boats, salaries, and other annual expenses if we could halve the number of summers necessary to accomplish the same amount of work. There were two approaches: (1) to increase the number of hours of under-water work each summer so that the necessary 1000 to 1500 hours could be squeezed into two campaigns, or (2) to increase the amount of work done during each hour on the sea bed so that the next wreck would take fewer hours to excavate. We tried both approaches with success.

First we increased the number of man-hours on the sea bottom each summer both by enlarging the diving staff and making longer dives. The latter was made possible by the use of a submersible decompression chamber, an air-filled steel sphere into which divers could swim to decompress for long periods of time in dry comfort at various depths; now divers could decompress for up to an hour at a time, something we would not ask them to do twice a day in open water [Pl. 62]. During decompression we sometimes breathed pure oxygen, which decreased the required decompression time. Thus, although the new wreck was 120 to 140 feet deep, we were making dives as long or longer than those we had made on the Byzantine wreck.

While increasing the number of hours on the site, we also increased the amount of work done during each hour. A high-pressure water jet and a huge aluminium air lift mounted on seventy feet of 'railroad track' along the lower side of the wreck were helpful in removing sand, but both were later abandoned in favour of numerous light and portable air lifts of PVC plastic which Katzev was already using on his site. Mapping of the well-preserved wooden hull was done entirely by stereophotogrammetry, with a specially designed camera on the bar above the site. On the surface we now had the advantage of multiplex mapping equipment borrowed from the Office of Naval Research. This complex system allowed us to draw accurate plans, with elevations, directly from projected stereo-slides of the wreck: one slide was projected in red and the other in blue onto a tracing table which could be moved up and down with a calibrated screw mechanism; by wearing glasses with one red and one blue lens, the operator could follow the lines of the hull with his pencil by moving the table up and down just enough to keep a point of light projected from beneath the table always resting directly on the surface of the wood [Fig. 47].

With these new techniques, we all but finished the excavation of the deeper Roman ship in only two summers, even though it proved to be imbedded in a far thicker layer of sand than we had previously encountered.

Meanwhile fresh faces were introducing fresh ideas, and already Katzev has developed a number of important innovations for full-scale excavations. One of these is his 'underwater telephone booth', a plexiglass hemisphere mounted on legs and filled with air from the surface [Pl. 29]. These were used at both Kyrenia and Yassi Ada with great success, and have since been adopted by professional diving groups unconcerned with archaeology. Not only can divers communicate easily with their colleagues above, by telephones inside, but their ability to stand in fresh air from their chests up has already prevented panic and potential accidents. If a diver runs out of air at a depth of 140 feet, it is certainly much easier to swim a few feet to a phone booth than to have to worry about getting to the surface; once inside he can change to a full tank, discuss the problem with his diving partner, and alert the barge above if necessary.

Katzev also took the time to make a preliminary survey of his site with probes, a metal detector, and a proton magnetometer.

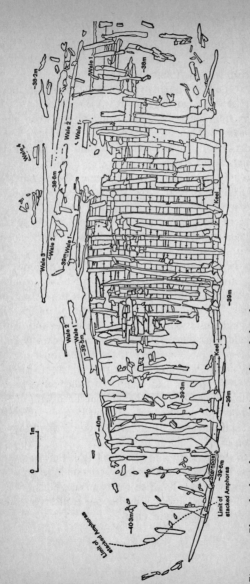

Figure 47. Plan of a fourth-century shipwreck made by photogrammetry

These gave him a better idea of what lay under the sand and enabled him to place his gridwork above the site with greater accuracy than we had attained earlier.

The excavations at Kyrenia and Yassi Ada were concluded only within weeks of this writing, and it is too early to draw scientific conclusions from them; years of study of the wood and other objects remain. But one unmistakable conclusion has come out of our experiences: in underwater excavation the most important concern is always safety.

By 1969 only Eric Ryan, Yüksel Eğdemir, Claude Duthuit, and I of the original staff at Cape Gelidonya were still diving in Turkey. A week after he had arrived at Yassi Ada, Ryan made a routine ascent from the wreck up the slope to the submersible decompression chamber about fifty yards away. Without warning, and for reasons still not known, he passed out twenty feet below the surface from an air embolism. In less than ten minutes he was recovering on Yassi Ada in a four-man, double-lock recompression chamber outfitted with oxygen breathing equipment. This was possible only because of an alert and fit diving partner; an elaborate communications network of telephones and radios linking the island, the submersible chamber, the wreck, and the diving barge, with permanent watches at the radios ready to call for a boat or the doctor; and an excellent staff which, under the direction of Laurence Joline, had familiarized themselves with emergency chamber procedures. Joline had not dived with us since his own decompression accident in 1961, but he had continued as an important staff member, constantly urging still greater safety measures on us.

All of this equipment and personnel took time and money to assemble, but no excavation under water should be done without a similar arrangement. Ryan still uses a cane, but he was lucky. Had he suffered the embolism during our earlier years he would have been dead a few minutes later.

9. THE FUTURE

UNDERWATER archaeology, as has been shown
in the previous chapters, differs from that on dry land only in its
methods, and its future is closely tied to advances in diving and
underwater technology. A few facts gleaned from the shipwrecks
now known in the Mediterranean reveal the present limitations
of underwater archaeology, and indicate the promise of what may
lie in the future.

In spite of the many references in antiquity to ships going
down in storms and in battles near identified points, not one of
the Classical wrecks so far excavated was found as the result of a
scientific search such as that which led to the finding of the Vasa
and various other later wrecks; all were chance discoveries of
fishermen, sports divers, and spongers. The sea is simply far too
large to be surveyed for ancient wrecks by divers swimming beneath the waves. The expedition which first dived on the Bronze
Age shipwreck at Cape Gelidonya, even with quite accurate
directions from the sponge diver who found it, took days to spot
the almost invisible remains beneath concretion and sea growth.
Relatively shallow and often broken artifacts may be found scattered over dangerous reefs, such as that at Yassi Ada, but it will
need both perseverance and luck to locate the better preserved and
deeper ships near by.

Sonar, both side-scanning and mud-penetrating, underwater
television, core samplers, magnetometers, metal detectors, submersibles – all these have proved successful in searching for wrecks
in various parts of the world. It is now time to use them in a
carefully planned programme over a period of years, calling on
the cooperation of many institutions and specialists. Perhaps the
goal should be to locate one of the triremes which made Athens
great. Even if a trireme were not found for many years, other
equally important wrecks would surely come to light, and the
experience would lead to the development and refinement of still

better search techniques – including, perhaps, such devices a
acoustic imaging systems now being developed to make 'phot-
graphs' with sound waves.

None of the wrecks excavated in the Mediterranean lay a
depths of two hundred feet or more, yet sponge draggers con
stantly pull up pottery and metal in their nets from much greate
depths, and already we know the locations of sites approachin
three hundred feet. Their scientific exploitation will also depen
on modern technology. Submarines will allow archaeologists t
map the visible remains with stereophotography and to clear awa
the sand with portable, neutrally buoyant air lifts directed by r
motely controlled manipulators attached to the submarines. Onc
the objects in the ancient cargoes have been recorded *in situ*, the
will be placed into lifting baskets and hauled or ballooned to th
surface.

Only one thing is missing, and that is the sure touch of th
archaeologist's hand on the site. The present scientific controvers
over whether manned or unmanned vehicles are more practic
in the exploration of outer space is easily answered for th
archaeological exploration of inner space : only a vast array c
the most delicate manipulators imaginable could clean and rais
the fragile and fragmentary pieces of wood which are so easil
and gently handled by human divers.

Again, scientific advances during the past few years indica
that the time is not far off when the archaeologist will be ab
to work as a diver on almost any site in the Mediterranean. Mixe
gas diving, such as that which substitutes helium for most of th
nitrogen in the diver's air, already allows divers to go deep
without suffering from narcosis, and other mixtures will redu
the likelihood of 'the bends'. Hannes Keller, a young Swiss math
matician, has dived to one thousand feet with an undisclosed ga
mixture; the experiment ended with the tragic death of h
diving partner Peter Small, seemingly because of an equipmen
failure, but Keller's survival proved the applicability of h
theories. C.O.M.E.X., a professional diving firm in Marseille, ha
simulated even deeper dives, and several companies are developir
mixed-gas scuba equipment that will make similar dives in ope
water commonplace.

Probably as important for the future of underwater archaeology are the underwater houses now being developed. Based on the principle that pressurized gases (usually a special mixture rather than plain air) are not harmful as long as the diver stays under pressure, these houses have openings below and act as bubbles of entrapped air on the sea-bed. Divers can enter and leave freely through these openings in the house floors while living and work- ing on the bottom for days or weeks at a time; they do not risk 'the bends' until the extremely long decompression periods which follow their stays under water. Captain Cousteau has already built an experimental village beneath the Red Sea, in which men lived for a month at about 35 feet, with two staying in a lower house at 90 feet for a week; the two men in the deeper house could swim down and work at 165 feet and return to their 'home' for eating and sleeping. Even the garage for Cousteau's submarine was under water, so that its two-man crew could take trips to one thousand feet without ever coming to the surface for servicing the tiny vessel. Since then, on the French Riviera, Cousteau has had men living in houses at depths of 330 feet and 600 feet.

Edwin Link, whose work at Port Royal and Caesarea has been mentioned earlier (pp. 85–6), has turned his technical ability to the same problems. In June of 1964 he placed an inflated rubber house 430 feet beneath the sea in the Bahamas, where the Belgian diver Robert Stenuit and Jon Lindbergh, son of the famous pioneer in flying, remained for two days. The following month, U.S. Navy divers under the direction of Captain George Bond, spent eleven days living in and diving from a steel capsule 192 feet down; the planned stay of three weeks was cut short by a threatening storm, which endangered the surface tender, but the experiment paved the way for astronaut Scott Carpenter's month-long stay at 205 feet in 1965.

The day is not far off when archaeologists will live in such houses and, working in shifts, will be able to excavate even through the night with their sites lit up by flood-lights. A wreck such as the Byzantine ship at Yassi Ada would then require one summer at most for its full investigation, rather than the four summers needed with ordinary divers whose time was so limited.

Where underwater houses are not practicable, excavators will be lowered from surface vessels in pressurized 'personnel transfer capsules' (P.T.C.'s) which they will leave wearing mixed-gas scuba equipment. After working for several hours on a site, wearing specially heated suits, they will re-enter the P.T.C. to be raised and locked into a deck decompression chamber (D.D.C.) to eat, sleep, and work – always under pressure – until time for their next dive. As in the underwater house, they will waste time decompressing only once, at the end of several days.

Edwin Link has gone so far as to combine a P.T.C. with a submarine. His revolutionary submersible *Deep Diver* has carried men to depths of more than 500 feet, where they were locked out into open water to perform experimental tasks. Later they re-entered the submarine and began their decompression while *Deep Diver* returned to her support ship on the surface. It was even possible to lift the submarine from the water and lock it onto a large D.D.C. in order that the men would have more room and comfort while decompressing.

Still further advances in diving can now hardly be imagined but Captain Cousteau has already spoken with great seriousness of the progress being made in space science to relieve the lungs completely of their work. Blood will be diverted through a regenerating capsule worn by the diver and, with his lungs filled with an incompressible fluid, the future *homo aquaticus* will be able to dive to thousands of feet without breathing and without, therefore, suffering any of the dangers of 'the bends' or narcosis. If this seems fantastic, one need only remember that during the first experiments with the steam locomotive there were many people who thought that the human body would not be able to withstand the acceleration of a train.

Underwater houses and submarines for archaeology sound terribly costly, but expenses are relative. Museums pay more for single works of Classical art than was spent for the submarine *Asherah*, which it is hoped will present to the world entire cargoes of such art. The cost of the Cape Gelidonya excavation was minuscule when compared to the salaries of scholars who have written so many now obsolete pages on the question of Semitic maritime influence in the Aegean Bronze Age. And a *Vasa* could not have been found at any price on land.

Many historical problems may be answered by the discovery and excavation of one or two shipwrecks. Answers to questions in the narrow field of Greek prehistory alone should be startling. Obsidian was brought from the island of Melos to the Greek mainland even before the use of pottery in the earliest Neolithic periods; what kinds of boats carried the obsidian, and who manned them? The answers lie beneath the waves. During thousands of years the cultures of Neolithic Greece changed suddenly more than once, and the last culture was overcome by new people at the beginning of the Early Bronze Age. If these people invaded or migrated by sea, some of their ships will have sunk during their voyages, and the discovery of these will provide clues to their origin that could not be found on numerous land digs. If Middle Bronze Age people came to Greece by sea, then we should find ships carrying the typical grey 'Minyan' pottery so closely associated with them, and the pottery might be found with other artifacts whose origin is determinable. With the Gelidonya wreck we have seen already what unexpected knowledge one site can reveal about sea trade in the Mediterranean during the Late Bronze Age, and at least two similar sites are known to exist. Finally, in the Iron Age, we may be able to identify the ships which carried the bronze griffin heads which are found on land from Turkey to the Etruscan tombs of Italy.

For later periods of antiquity it is obvious that our greatest knowledge of ancient sea-borne commerce, naval weapons, ship construction, harbour works, and daily life on ships will come from under water, but there is equally important information to be gained from cargoes alone. If most of the known monumental Greek bronzes have come from the sea at a time when underwater archaeology is still in its infancy, the promise for the future is clear. Ships have sunk every year since man first floated down a river on a raft, and it is evident that before long a shipwreck of at least every generation of reasonable antiquity will be discovered; later, generations will be reduced to decades. Those ships that contain cargoes datable by coins or other documents will offer

the best possible dating for some types of pottery and other arti
facts which are so important for dating strata in land excavations
New knowledge of ancient metallurgy, numismatics, metrology
and architecture, as well as sculpture, has resulted already from
underwater excavations, and other areas of archaeology will surely
profit as well. We have seen, moreover, that underwater
archaeology is not limited to the Mediterranean, nor to Classical
times.

The future of any field depends on the people in that field
Advances in diving techniques will be made by the inventive
geniuses of every generation, but the future of underwater
archaeology lies also in the hands of the archaeologists who must
use their new tools. One of the primary purposes of the Yassi Ada
excavation was the training of archaeology students, who were
advised to receive training in land excavation as well; already
three of the young archaeologists from that site have been in
charge of other underwater projects, and meanwhile all have
excavated on land. More of such training is needed, and it is hoped
that scholars specializing in all branches of archaeology soon
will observe and assist in the excavation of underwater sites. Then
whenever a site is discovered, regardless of its type, place or period
there will be a specialist, rather than simply an 'underwater
archaeologist' of undetermined interests, to supervise its excava
tion, even though the staff should include experienced member
to ensure safety. Of great value, too, will be the conservationist
who attack the problems of preserving water-soaked finds.

Diving and the use of underwater tools can be learned during
summers in the field, but techniques of excavation, on land o
under water, are but a small part of archaeology. The archaeologis
who excavates a Classical acropolis will have had sound training
in architecture, epigraphy, and pottery types, and his historica
knowledge of the period will be great; likewise, the excavator o
a Neolithic mound will be well versed in prehistory and its un
answered problems. Until recently, however, most underwate
excavators lacked academic training in the special problems thei
work might solve. More university seminars should be offered
in ancient maritime activities so that students can, along with

heir other courses, discuss aspects of naval warfare, ship con-
truction, and ancient trade-routes.

With this combination of technical achievement and academic
nterest, underwater archaeology will mature quickly. From
dvances during only the past decade, we may be sure that its
right future is certain.

BIBLIOGRAPHY

THIS bibliography is intended for the general reader, for archaeology under water embraces a large number of specialized fields. Anyone seriously interested in diving, for example, can keep abreast of current developments in such publications as the *American Journal of Physiology*, and should follow the proceedings of various conferences on diving physiology; the U.S. Navy Experimental Diving Unit in Washington, D.C., publishes such reports as *Decompression Sickness among Divers, An analysis of 935 cases*, by J. C. Rivera. Of interest, too, should be such books as *Dangerous Marine Animals* (Cambridge, Md., 1959) by Bruce Halstead, or *Sharks and Survival* (New York, 1964) edited by Perry Gilbert.

Articles on underwater photography appear in a vast number of journals, and for underwater photogrammetry alone one must consult articles in *Surveying and Mapping*, *Photogrammetric Engineering*, and *Missiles and Rockets*, to name but several of the more recent. Knowledge of new equipment may be gained from *Under Sea Technology*, but other sources are numerous; the bibliography for the relatively simple air lift, as shown in F. Dumas' *Deep-Water Archaeology*, runs to more than a hundred titles.

Reports of underwater research and finds pertaining strictly to archaeology have appeared in the following archaeological journals: *American Antiquity*, *American Journal of Archaeology*, *Les annales archéologiques de Syrie*, *Annual of the British School at Athens*, *Antiquity*, *Antiquity and Survival*, *Archaeology*, *Archäologische Anzeiger*, *Biblical Archaeologist*, *Bulletin de correspondence hellénique*, *Estudios de Cultura Maya*, *Expedition* (Bulletin of the University Museum of the University of Pennsylvania), *Gallia*, *Israel Exploration Journal*, *Klio*, *Monuments Piot*, *Pennsylvania Archaeologist*, *Proceedings of the Prehistoric Society*, *Revue archéologique*, *Revue des études grecques*, *Rivisti di Studi Liguri*, and the *Wisconsin Archaeologist*; every archaeologist can undoubtedly add to this list. *Studies in Conservation* carries articles of special interest to the discoverer of artifacts under water.

Reports and articles on underwater archaeology often appear in magazines devoted to diving, such as: *L'aventure sous-marine* (Paris),

Cris (Barcelona), Delphin (Hamburg), Mondo Sommerso (Rome), Neptun (Stuttgart), Skin Diver (Lynwood, Cal.), and Triton (London). Most underwater finds of consequence have been noted in the Illustrated London News, and some have been described in greater detail in Natural History Magazine, Scientific American, and the Geographical Magazine (England); accounts of a wide variety of underwater excavations of importance appear in the National Geographic Magazine (U.S.).

ABBREVIATIONS

A.A.	American Antiquity
A.J.A.	American Journal of Archaeology
I.L.N.	Illustrated London News
Nat.Geog.M.	National Geographic Magazine
S.A.	Scientific American
U.S.Nav.Inst.Proc.	United States Naval Institute Proceedings

CHAPTER 1

Sir Mortimer Wheeler, Archaeology from the Earth (Oxford, 1954).

Marine Archaeology, Developments during sixty years in the Mediterranean (London, 1965), edited by Joan du Plat Taylor. Reports of the major underwater excavations until 1960, many translated from French and Italian.

Diving into the Past: Theories, Techniques, and Applications of Underwater Archaeology (St Paul, Minnesota, 1964). The valuable proceedings of the Conference on Underwater Archaeology sponsored by the Minnesota Historical Society in 1963.

Atti del II Congresso Internazionale di Archeologia Sottomarina, Albenga 1958 (Bordighera, 1961). Useful papers, mostly in French and Italian, on pioneering excavations and surveys, nearly all in the Mediterranean.

Mendel Peterson, History Under the Sea. A Handbook for Underwater Explorations (Washington, D.C., 1965). Especially important for wreck surveyors and excavators in the Western Hemisphere, with excellent sections on identification and preservation of finds.

Philippe Diolé, Promenades d'archéologie sous-marine (Paris, 1952); 4000 Years Under the Sea, Excursions in Undersea Archaeology (London, 1954).

Suzanne de Borhegyi, Ships, Shoals, and Amphoras: the Story of

Underwater Archaeology (New York, 1961). For only slightly younger readers.

John Goggin, 'Underwater Archaeology, Its Nature and Limitations', *A.A.* 25 (1960) 348–54.

Peter Throckmorton, 'Ship Archaeology in the Aegean', *U.S.Nav.Inst. Proc.* 90 (Dec. 1964) 60–68.

CHAPTER 2

U.S. Department of the Navy, *Navy Diving Manual;* Navships 250–538 (Washington, D.C., 1959). Essential on any underwater excavation. Divers from other countries may prefer *Royal Naval Diving Manual* (London) or *La Plongée* (Paris).

P. Tailliez, F. Dumas, J.-Y. Cousteau, *et al.*, *The Complete Manual of Free Diving* (New York, 1957). An English translation of *La Plongée*.

The New Science of Skin and Scuba Diving (New York, 1957). An excellent beginning book by a committee of authorities.

Captain Stanley Miles, R.N., *Underwater Medicine* (London, 1962).

James Dugan, *Man Under the Sea* (New York, 1956), in England titled *Man Explores the Sea* (Harmondsworth, 1960). An authoritative and most readable history of all types of underwater activities, with a good chapter on underwater archaeology.

Jacques-Yves Cousteau, with Frederic Dumas, *The Silent World* (London, 1953; New York, 1956). The classic account of the beginnings of aqualung diving, prepared with the assistance of James Dugan.

Jacques-Yves Cousteau, with James Dugan, *The Living Sea* (London, New York, 1963).

Dimitri Rebikoff and Paul Cherney, *A Guide to Underwater Photography* (New York, 1957).

J. Greenberg, *Underwater Photography Simplified* (2nd ed., Coral Gables, Florida, 1963).

Encyclopédie du monde sous-marin (Paris, 1957).

CHAPTER 3

R. Forrest-Webb, 'The Challenge of the River Thames', *Triton* (November-December 1963) 16–18.

Donald P. Jewell, 'Fresh Water Archaeology'. *A.A.* 26 (1961) 414–16.

Robert C. Wheeler, 'History below the Rapids', *Minnesota History* 38 (1962) 24–34. 'Diving into the Past', *Canadian Geographical Journal* 65 (1962) 39–49.

Sigurd F. Olson, 'Relics from the Rapids', Nat.Geog.M. 124 (September 1963), 412–35.

Stephan F. de Borghegyi, 'From the Depths of Lake Amatitlan', I.L.N. v. 233, no. 6214 (1958) 70–72; 'Hallazgos Arqueologicos en Aguas del Lago de Amatitlan', Revista del Instituto de Antropologia e Historia de Guatemala 10 (1958) 3–12; 'Underwater Archaeology in the Maya Highlands', S.A. v. 200, no. 3 (March 1959) 100–13; 'Exploration in Lake Peten Itza', Archaeology 16 (1963) 14–24.

Bob Marx, 'Columbus' Last Two Ships Found in Jamaica', Argosy (September 1968) 32ff.

Anders Franzén, The Warship Vasa: Deep Diving and Marine Archaeology in Stockholm (Stockholm, 1960); 'Ghost from the Depths: The Warship Vasa', Nat.Geog.M. 121 (January 1962) 42–57.

Peter Throckmorton, The Lost Ships (Boston, 1964); 'Thirty-three Centuries Under the Sea', Nat.Geog.M. 117 (May 1960) 682–703.

R. Fernald, 'Techniques de recherche sous-marine', Archeologia 17 (July–August 1967) 34–35.

G. F. Bass and L. T. Joline, 'Problems of Deep Wreck Identification', Expedition 11, no. 1 (Fall 1968) 9–11.

G. F. Bass and D. M. Rosencrantz, A Diversified Program for the Study of Shallow Water Searching and Mapping Techniques (1968). Report submitted to the Office of Naval Research; available as report number AD 686 487, Clearinghouse (C.F.S.T.I.), Springfield, Virginia 22151.

CHAPTER 4

Guido Ucelli, Le Navi di Nemi (Rome, 1950).

G. D. van der Heide, 'Archaeological Investigations on New Land', Antiquity and Survival 3 (1955) 221–52.

Olaf Olsen and Ole Crumlin-Pedersen, Vikingeskibene I, Roskilde Fjord (Copenhagen, 1962–63); O. Crumlin-Pedersen, 'Viking Ships', The Undersea Challenge: Proceedings of the Second World Congress of Underwater Activities, London, 1962 (London, 1963) 88–98.

Robert S. Skerrett, 'Wreck of the Royal Savage Recovered', U.S.Nav. Inst.Proc. 61 (1935) 1646–52.

L. F. Hagglund, 'The Continental Gondola Philadelphia', U.S.Nav.Inst. Proc. 62 (1936) 665–9.

'The Cairo Story', Special Section of the Vicksburg Evening Post,

Vicksburg, Mississippi (11 December 1964); 'Resurrection of ar Ironclad', *Life* 58 (12 February 1965) 41–4.

Edwin C. Bearss, *Hardluck Ironclad, the Sinking and Salvage of the Cairo* (Louisiana State University Press, 1966).

C. O. Cederlund, *The Warship Vasa, Exhibition Wasavaret* (Stockholm, 1963).

Bengt Ohrelius, *Vasa, the king's ship* (London, 1962).

CHAPTER 5

Stanley J. Olsen, 'Scuba as an Aid to Archaeologists and Paleontologists', *Curator*, American Museum of Natural History, 4 (1961) 371–8; 'Underwater Treasure', *Florida Wildlife* 15, no. 11 (April 1962).

Alfred M. Tozzer, *Chichen Itza and its Cenote of Sacrifice*, Memoirs of the Peabody Museum, vols. 11 and 12 (Cambridge, Mass., 1957)

Samuel K. Lothrop, *Metals from the Cenote of Sacrifice, Chichen Itza, Yucatan*, Memoirs of the Peabody Museum, vol. 10 (Cambridge, Mass., 1952).

E. D. Hurtado and Bates Littlehales, 'Into the Well of Sacrifice', I and II, *Nat.Geog.M.* 120 (October 1961) 540–61.

E. Wyllys Andrews, 'Excavations at Dzibilchaltun, Northwestern Yucatan, Mexico', *Proc. of the American Philosophical Society* 104 (June 1960) 254–65.

Luis Marden, 'Up from the Well of Time', *Nat.Geog.M.* 115 (January 1959) 110–29.

A. Merlin, 'Submarine Discoveries in the Mediterranean', *Antiquity* 4 (1930) 405–14.

S. Casson, 'Submarine Research in Greece', *Antiquity* 13 (1939) 80–6.

G. Karo, 'Art Salvaged from the Sea', *Archaeology* 1 (1948) 179–85.

G. Weinberg, *et al.*, 'The Antikythera Shipwreck Reconsidered', *Trans. Am. Phil. Soc.*, N.S. 55, pt. 3 (1965).

Derek Price, 'An Ancient Greek Computer', *S.A.* 200, no. 6 (June 1959) 60–67.

Werner Fuchs, *Der Schiffsfund von Mahdia* (Tübingen, 1963).

Philippe Tailliez, *Nouvelles plongées sans câble* (Paris, 1960).

Bosch Gimpera, 'Huelva', in Ebert's *Reallexikon der Vorgeschichte*; original account in *Boletin de la R. Academia de la Historia* 83 (1923) 89–91.

CHAPTER 6

A. Poidebard, 'Un grand port disparu : Tyr. Recherches aériennes et sous-marines, 1934–6', *Biblio. arch. et hist.* 29 (Paris, 1939).

A. Poidebard and J. Lauffray, *Sidon. Aménagements antiques du port de Saida. Études aériennes, au sol et sous-marines,* 1946–50 (Beirut, 1951).

Nicholas Flemming, 'Underwater Adventure in Apollonia' and 'Apollonia Revisited', *Geographical Magazine* 31 (February 1959) 497–508, and 33 (January 1961) 522–30.

Kenneth MacLeish, 'Sea Search into History at Caesarea', *Life* 50 (5 May 1961) 72–82.

Honor Frost, *Under the Mediterranean* (London and Englewood Cliffs, N.J., 1963); 'Rouad, ses récifs et mouillages', *Les annales archéologiques de Syrie* 14 (1964) 67–74.

John C. Hawthorne, 'Cenchreae, Port of Corinth', *Archaeology* 18 (1965) 191–200.

Vianor Pachulia, 'Soviet Archaeology: The Search for Lost Dioscuria in the Eastern Black Sea', *I.L.N.* 244 (25 April 1964) 644–5.

Spiridon Marinatos, 'Helice: A Submerged Town of Classical Greece', *Archaeology* 13 (1960) 186–93.

Elisha Linder and Olivier Leenhardt, 'Recherches d'archéologie sous-marine sur la côte mediterranéenne d'Israel', *Revue archéologique* (January–March 1964) 47–51.

Marion Clayton Link, 'Exploring the Drowned City of Port Royal', *Nat.Geog.M.* 117 (February 1960) 151–83.

Gerhard Kapitän, 'Vorläufiger Bericht über die Untersuchungen an der Kemlade in Cambser See, Kr. Schwerin', *Ausgrabungen und Funde* 6 (1961) 205–10; 'Das Raubritternest im See', *Neptun* (December 1964) 307–10.

Gerhard Kapitän, 'Schiffsfrachten antiker Baugesteine und Architekturteile vor den Küsten Ostsiziliens', *Klio* 39 (1961) 276–318; 'Neue archäologische Unterwasserforschungen vor den Küsten Ostsiziliens', *Delphin* (Four monthly issues, December 1962–March 1963).

P. Merifield and D. M. Rosencrantz, 'A Simple Method for Surveying A Small Area Underwater'. *Limnology and Oceanography* 11, no. 3 (1966) 408–9.

Peter Throckmorton and John Bullitt, 'Underwater Surveys in Greece: 1962,' *Expedition* 5 (Winter 1963) 16–23.

John B. Ward-Perkins and Peter Throckmorton, 'The San Pietro Wreck', *Archaeology* 18 (1965) 201–9.

Roberto Dei and Sacha de Fé, '27 Ancore in un Cucchiaio', *Mondo Sommerso* (November 1964), 87–99.

Alexander de Fé, 'Mystery Find at the Galli Islands', *Triton* (January 1965) 38–41.

Eric Ryan and G. F. Bass, 'Underwater Surveying and Draughting – A Technique', *Antiquity* 36 (1962) 252–61.

Gianni Roghi, 'Note tecniche sul rilevamento e lo scavo della nave romana di Spargi', *Bollettino e Atti* (Centro Italiano de Ricercatori Subacquei, 1958–59) 9–20. 'La seconda campagna di scavi sotto marina sulla nave romana di Spargi (Sardegna)', *Rivista di Studi Liguri* 25 (1959) 301–2.

G. F. Bass, 'The *Asherah*: A Submarine for Archaeology', *Archaeology* 18 (1965) 7–14.

P. Merifield, R. Karius, and D. Rosencrantz, 'Stereo-Mapping of Underwater Terrain from a Submarine', *Ocean Science and Engineering*, Trans. of the Joint Conference, Marine Technology Soc. and Am. Soc. of Limnology and Oceanography, Washington, D.C., June 1965.

CHAPTER 7

Ferdinand Keller, *The Lake Dwellings of Switzerland and other Parts of Europe* (London, 1866).

Homer L. Ferguson, *Salvaging Revolutionary Relics from the York River* (Newport News, Virginia, 1939).

Robert Brill, 'The Record of Time in Weathered Glass', *Archaeology* 14 (1961) 18–22.

Nino Lamboglia, 'La nave romana di Albenga', *Revue d'études Ligures* 18 (1952) 131–236; 'Diario di scavo a bordo dell "Artiglio"', *Inguana e Intemelia* 5, no. 1 (1950) 1–8.

Jacques-Yves Cousteau, 'Fish Men Discover a 2,200-Year-Old Greek Ship', *Nat.Geog.M.* 105 (January 1954) 1–36.

Fernand Benoît, *L'épave du Grand Congloué à Marseille; Gallia* suppl. 14 (Paris 1961).

Willy Haag, 'Recherches archéologiques sur les palafittes du lac de Neuchâtel', *L'aventure sous-marine* 36 (December 1961–January 1962) 288 ff.

Guy de Frondeville, *Les visiteurs de la mer* (Paris, 1956).

F. Dumas, 'Le Dramont: troisième chantier français d'archéologie sous-marine', *Études et sports sous-marins* 6 (1959) 15; A. Sivirine, 'Particularités du travail sous-marin sur l'épave du Dramont', *Le plongeur et l'archéologie* (Confédération Mondiales des Activités Sub-aquatiques) (Paris, 1960) 23–5.

G. F. Bass, 'Underwater Excavations at Yassi Ada: A Byzantine Shipwreck', *Archäologischer Anzeiger* (1962) 537–64.

F. Dumas, *Deep-Water Archaeology* (London, 1962).

F. Dumas, *Épaves antiques* (Paris, 1964).

G. F. Bass, 'The Cape Gelidonya Wreck: Preliminary Report', A.J.A. 65 (1961) 267–76; *Cape Gelidonya: A Bronze Age Shipwreck, Trans. Am. Phil. Soc.* N.S. 57, pt. 8 (1967).

Peter Throckmorton, 'Oldest Known Shipwreck Yields Bronze Age Cargo', *Nat.Geog.M.* 121 (May 1962) 696–711.

CHAPTER 8

G. F. Bass, 'Underwater Archaeology: Key to History's Warehouse', *Nat.Geog.M.* 124 (July 1963) 138–56; 'Bodrum Yassiada Sualti Kazilari (1961)', *Türk Arkeoloji Dergisi* 12 (1962) 8–11.

M. Katzev and F. van Doorninck, 'Replicas of Iron Tools from a Byzantine Shipwreck', *Studies in Conservation* 11, pt. 3 (1966) 133–42.

Ray M. Seborg and Robert B. Inverarity, 'Conservation of 200-year-old Water-logged Boats with Polyethylene Glycol', *Studies in Conservation* 7 (November 1962) 111–20.

H. Muller-Beck and A. Haas, 'A Method of Wood Preservation Using Arigal C', *Studies in Conservation* 5 (November 1960) 150–58.

F. van Doorninck, 'Reconstruction d'un navire byzantine du VIIe siècle, *Archeologia* 17 (July–August 1967) 38.

G. F. Bass, 'Pour un meilleur rendement des techniques de fouilles sous-marines', *Archeologia* 17 (July–August 1967) 33; 'New Tools for Undersea Archaeology', *Nat.Geog.M.* 134 (September 1968) 402–423; 'The Turkish Aegean: Proving Ground for Underwater Archaeology', *Expedition* 10, pt. 3 (Spring 1968) 3–10.

G. F. Bass and M. L. Katzev, 'New Tools for Underwater Archaeology', *Archaeology* 21, pt. 3 (June 1968) 165–73.

Peter Throckmorton, 'Ancient Shipwreck Yields New Facts – And a Strange Cargo', *Nat.Geog.M.* 135, pt. 2 (February 1969).

J. N. Green, E. T. Hall, and M. L. Katzev, 'Survey of a Greek Shipwreck off Kyrenia, Cyprus', *Archaeometry* 10 (1967) 47–56.

CHAPTER 9

John A. Pritzlaff and Richard E. Munske, 'Manned Submersibles of the World', *Undersea Technology* (August 1964) 20–26.

Jacques-Yves Cousteau, 'At Home in the Sea', *Nat.Geog.M.* 125 (April 1964) 465–507.

Edwin A. Link, 'Our Man-in-Sea Project', and Lord Kilbracken, 'The Long Deep Dive', *Nat.Geog.M.* 123 (May 1963) 712–31; Edwin Link, 'Outpost Under the Ocean', and Robert Stenuit, 'The Deepest Days', *ibid.* 127 (April 1965) 530–47.

James Atwater and Roger Vaughan, 'Room at the Bottom of the Sea', *Saturday Evening Post* (5 September 1964) 18–25.

H. A. O'Neal, *et al.*, An Experimental Eleven-Day Undersea Saturation Dive at 193 Feet. Sealab I Project Report (Office of Naval Research, Washington, D.C., 14 June 1965).

J.-Y. Cousteau, 'Working for Weeks on the Sea Floor', *Nat.Geog.M.* 129, no. 4 (April 1966) 498–537.

K. MacLeish and B. Littlehales, 'A Taxi for the Deep Frontier', *Nat. Geog.M.* 133, no. 1 (January 1968) 139–50.

James Dugan, *et al.*, *World Beneath the Sea* (National Geographic Society, Washington, D.C., 1967).

Jacques-Yves Cousteau, 'The Era of "Homo Aquaticus",' *The Undersea Challenge*, Second World Congress of Underwater Activities (London, 1963) 8–11.

Fernand Benoît, 'La création d'un Institut d'Archéologie Navale' *L'aventure sous-marine* 21 (June–July 1959).

NOTES ON THE PLATES

Attendant closes the face plate of a helmeted diver who is about to descend on the American Civil War gunboat *Cairo*, sunk in the Yazoo River, Mississippi, in 1862. Courtesy *Vicksburg Evening Post*, Vicksburg, Miss.

A helmeted Turkish sponge diver examines the remains of a late Roman ship, whose cargo of terra-cotta tiles now rests 70 feet under the Aegean Sea. The diver holds a net bag for gathering sponges; his air hose and life line run to a small boat which follows his bubbles on the surface. Mustafa Kapkin.

A four-man, double-lock Galeazzi recompression chamber of the type built for the University of Pennsylvania Museum in 1965. The air lock allows the expedition doctor to enter the chamber, give medical treatment to a stricken diver, and leave. Such a chamber can treat the most serious cases of 'the bends'.

A diver, with hookah or narghile hose trailing behind him, jumps from a sponge boat into the water at Cape Gelidonya, Turkey. One hand keeps his mask in place, and the other holds an underwater metal-detector which is powered by batteries slung across the diver's back.

A scuba diver fights against the rapids of the Granite River, on the Minnesota-Ontario border, in his search for artifacts lost by overturned voyageurs' canoes. Courtesy *National Geographic Magazine* © National Geographic Society.

A nest of brass and copper trade kettles found by divers in Minnesota's Horsetail Rapids. This discovery substantiated Dr E. W. Davis' belief that such goods, carried in canoes to the Indians in return for furs, would be found below such dangerous rapids. The kettles were given to the Minnesota Historical Society, which expanded the rewarding search. Courtesy Minnesota Historical Society.

Robert C. Wheeler (kneeling) and E. W. Davis (with hood) inspect a line of trade kettles just retrieved by diver Dennis Dalen, and his partners Donald Franklin and Curtis Anderson (not shown) from Horsetail Rapids, Minnesota, during the summer of 1960. Courtesy *Minneapolis Sunday Tribune*.

Wooden figure of a helmeted warrior from the stern section of the warship Vasa. Height 71 inches. Vasa Museum, Stockholm. From Anders Franzén's book on the Vasa.

9. Hollow three-pronged censer (3 prongs on top broken off) from Lake Amatitlan, Guatemala. Censer has six vertical flanges and depicts the Mexican Rain God, Tlaloc. Early or Middle Classic period A.D. 200-600. Height 23 inches. Milwaukee Public Museum Photo.

10. Effigy censer cover, from Lake Amatitlan, in shape of a jaguar god. Middle Classic Period A.D. 400-600. Height 10½ inches. Milwaukee Public Museum Photo.

11. Lake Amatitlan, Guatemala, 4,000 feet above sea-level. Maya offerings recovered from the lake by Manfred Töpke and his diving companions led to a full-scale survey of its water and shores by Stephan de Borhegyi and students from the San Carlos University in 1957 and 1958. Milwaukee Public Museum Photo.

12. The seventeenth-century warship Vasa in dry dock after being raised from the bottom of Stockholm Harbour by the Neptun Salvage Company. Absence of shipworms in the Baltic Sea allows such excellent preservation of wood. Photograph courtesy of Anders Franzén.

13. One of the two Roman 'pleasure barges' revealed by the draining of Lake Nemi, near Rome, between 1928 and 1931; divers had been salvaging wood and artifacts from the wrecks since at least as early as the fifteenth century. Supports keep the hull from settling and falling apart. From Guido Ucelli, Le Navi di Nemi.

14. The ironclad gunboat Cairo, before it was sunk by a mine in the Yazoo River, Mississippi, on 12 December 1862. Following its discovery in 1956, efforts were made to raise the vessel intact, but it was finally raised in three sections in 1965. Library of Congress photograph.

15. Air view of the sheet-steel coffer dam, enclosing 1600 square yards of Denmark's Roskilde Fjord, as it was pumped dry in 1962 to uncover five Viking ships. Courtesy Ole Crumlin-Pedersen of the National Museum, Denmark.

16. After nine centuries beneath a few feet of water, the stem of a Viking ship emerges. Large stones which held the ships down, presumably as a blockade against some now unknown enemy, had to be removed carefully as the water around the fragile wood was pumped out of the dammed area of Roskilde Fjord. Courtesy Ole Crumlin-Pedersen, National Museum, Denmark.

17. An air lift spouts water and artifacts which are caught in a special sieve floating on the water of the cenote at Chichen Itza, Mexico

Courtesy *National Geographic Magazine* © National Geographic Society.

18. Tula-Toltec warriors extract the heart of a Maya captive; the gold disc on which the scene is represented was raised from the *cenote* at Chichen Itza in northern Yucatan, and is one of ten discs showing scenes of a war between Tula-Toltec and Maya. Diameter 9 inches. Courtesy Peabody Museum, Harvard University.

19. Bronze Zeus or Poseidon found by Greek sponge divers in the sea near Cape Artemision in northern Euboea. It is one of only two monumental bronze statues existing from the fifth century B.C. Height 6 feet 10 inches. National Museum, Athens. Photograph by Alison Frantz.

20. Bronze boy netted in Marathon Bay in 1925; thought by some to be an original work by Praxiteles. Height 4 feet 3 inches. National Museum, Athens. Photograph by Alison Frantz.

21. The Piombino Apollo, probably an original bronze of the early fifth century B.C., but possibly a Roman creation. Netted by fishermen off the coast of Etruria in the early nineteenth century. Height 3 feet 9 inches. Louvre, Paris. Hirmer Fotoarchiv.

22. Statue of a youth salvaged from a ship wrecked off the island of Antikythera between 80 and 65 B.C. Already an antique at that time, it is the only large-scale bronze from the first quarter of the fourth century B.C. Height 6 feet 5 inches. National Museum, Athens. Photograph by Alison Frantz.

23. Bronze bust, possibly of Demeter, netted by a Turkish sponge dragger in 200 to 300 feet of water near Marmaris, Turkey. About life-size. Archaeological Museum, Izmir. Photograph by Mustafa Kapkin.

24. Negro youth in bronze, netted by a Turkish sponge dragger in around 300 feet of water during the summer of 1962. Underwater Archaeological Museum, Bodrum, Turkey. Courtesy Turkish Department of Antiquities. Photograph by Mustafa Kapkin.

25. At Cape Gelidonya, Turkey, the author holds a vertical range pole on a bench mark, while Claude Duthuit records the measurement just taken from the pole with a piece of string. Photograph by Herb Greer.

26. A diver swims over a brick wall which sank, along with two-thirds of Port Royal, Jamaica, during an earthquake in 1692; a crack in the wall holds tumbled artifacts. The lost city was explored in 1959 by an expedition directed by Edwin A. Link, and

sponsored by the National Geographic Society, Smithsonian Institution, and Institute of Jamaica. Courtesy *National Geographic Magazine* © National Geographic Society.

27. Nikos Kartelias and Roger Wallihan record some of the fourteen hundred measurements made on a cargo of granite columns found near Methone in southwestern Greece. Courtesy Peter Throckmorton.

28. The blocked out, but unfinished, garlands show clearly on one of the Roman sarcophagi which had been carried in a ship wrecked near Methone, Greece. John Bullitt records data on a sheet of plastic during an investigation under the supervision of the Hellenic Federation of Sub-aquatic Activities. Courtesy Peter Throckmorton.

29. Paul Fardig leaves an underwater telephone booth next to a fourth-century A.D. Roman wreck 130 feet deep. The clear plastic bubble is supplied with air through a hose to the surface, and divers may stand up inside with water rising only chest high. Photograph by John Cassils.

30. Differential depth gauge developed by Robert Love for precise elevation measurements of sea-bed topology and shipwreck artifacts. Designed to function hundreds of feet below the surface, this instrument measures within inches the relative depths of underwater points over any 30-foot depth increment independent of surface tidal changes. Photo courtesy Robert Love.

31. Mendel Peterson, Head Curator of the Department of Armed Forces History, Smithsonian Institution, records reading of bearing and distance used to plot parts of ancient shipwreck. This is the site of a ship of unknown nationality which was wrecked about 1595. The site has yielded a collection of gold, silver, gems and other artifacts to its discoverers, Teddy Tucker and Robert Canton of Bermuda. Smithsonian Institution photograph.

32. An underwater surveyor sights through the alidade on one of a pair of plane tables used to measure the Byzantine shipwreck at Yassi Ada, Turkey. The inquisitive fish lived on the wreck for the four years that it was being excavated by the University of Pennsylvania Museum. Courtesy *National Geographic Magazine* © National Geographic Society.

33. The Rolleimarin underwater camera hangs by gimbals from a horizontal metal bar floating 20 feet above the Byzantine shipwreck at Yassi Ada. The three lead weights attached to the camera case by iron 'legs' assure the correct position of the lens; to prevent moving the camera while taking a picture, Don Rosencrantz uses

a cable release made from a jeep choke cable. Only by such careful control can accurate stereo-pairs be made. Photo by Claude Duthuit.

34. Elevation measurements on fragments of hull planks are made by artist Eric Ryan from the grid on the base of a photographic tower. The base of the tower rests on one of the horizontal 'steps' of angle iron constructed over the Byzantine wreck at Yassi Ada. Numbered plastic labels identify pieces of wood and amphoras, still partially covered by sand. The wire lifting basket may be seen behind the grid. Photo by Jack Sofield.

35, 36 A stereo-pair made with a Rolleimarin camera by the method shown in Plate 33; all of the plastic identification labels could be read clearly, although the photographs were taken from more than 20 feet above the amphoras, with natural light at a depth of 120 feet. Elevation measurements calculated by this pair were in error because of the slight distortion caused by the difference between the indices of refraction of water and of air; the problem of distortion was later solved by using a camera with a water-correcting lens. Photographs by Donald Rosencrantz.

37. Julian Whittlesey measures the parallax on a pair of stereophotographs with a micrometer; the Zeiss Stereoscope allows him to study the remains of the Byzantine shipwreck in three dimensions. From his measurements he will be able to calculate the elevations of objects in the cargo and fragments of the wooden hull. Photo by Mustafa Kapkin.

38. Bearing the seal of the University of Pennsylvania on one side and the flag of the National Geographic Society on the other, the two-man submarine *Asherah* is named by Ann Bass on 28 May, 1964. The National Science Foundation also assisted in enabling the University to order this unique craft built by the Electric Boat Company of General Dynamics. The *Asherah* can descend to a depth of 600 feet and remain for up to ten hours while operating at speeds from one to four knots. Six ports provide visibility, a speaker on the front allows the submarine occupants to give directions to divers outside, and floodlights can be attached to electrical outlets in various places on the submarine.

39. Accompanied by a diver, the *Asherah* dives near Yassi Ada, Turkey. The metal frame bolted to the submarine normally supports the two aerial survey cameras seen in Plate 40, but they were not used on this dive. Two electric motors, one on either side of the hull, can be rotated to move the 4½-ton *Asherah* up, down, forward, or backward. The plexiglass bubble over the hatch fills with water when the submarine is submerged, but protects the open

hatch from breaking waves when on the surface. Courtesy *National Geographic Magazine* © National Geographic Society.

40. A pair of aerial survey cameras encased in underwater housings for use on the *Asherah*; the distortion-correcting Ivanoff lens seen on one of the cameras allowed accurate plans and sections to be made from stereo-pairs taken from the submarine. The electrical outlets seen on the other camera show that the cameras could be triggered electrically from within the *Asherah's* pressure hull; the cameras automatically advanced their own film and re-cocked their shutters after each picture. Built by Illinois Institute of Technology Research Institute.

41. The top of the air lift used at Yassi Ada, Turkey, was fitted with a wire basket which allowed most of the sand and mud sucked up through the tube to be carried away by the current; larger objects, trapped by the wire mesh, fell into the cloth bag below, which could be changed for an empty bag when full. Diver Waldemar Illing carries a full bag to the surface by means of a descending line running from the barge to the Byzantine wreck.

42. Water spouts from the 10-inch air lift used at Port Royal, Jamaica, and runs over a barge tied alongside Edwin A. Link's boat *Sea-Diver*. Marion Link, wife of the expedition director, receives a piece of pottery just salvaged by her son Clayton. Courtesy *National Geographic Magazine* © National Geographic Society.

43. The author holds the larger of two air lifts used at Cape Gelidonya, Turkey, while Gernolf Martens searches through the thin layer of sand near the air-lift mouth. Only the lower section of the air-lift tube, to which air was pumped from the surface through a small hose, was of reinforced flexible rubber. Photograph by Herb Greer.

44. Divers using air lift on Roman wreck at Ile du Levant. The wood was well preserved in places, but careful exploration revealed that it was not preserved far from the keel. Courtesy Philippe Tailliez.

45. Robert Stenuit, famous for his extended deep dives under the direction of Edwin Link, uses an underwater metal detector on the sea-bed off the coast of Sicily. Courtesy Gerhard Kapitän.

46. The core-sampler used at Yassi Ada, for prospecting the Byzantine wreck before excavation, proved too small to be effective; a larger core-sampler, used with care, could aid excavators on future sites. Photograph by Mustafa Kapkin.

47. Using a hammer and chisel, Claude Duthuit cuts around a mass

of concreted cargo on the Bronze Age shipwreck at Cape Gelidonya, Turkey. The photograph, taken with natural light at a depth of 90 feet, shows the extreme clarity of the Aegean along much of the Turkish coast. Photograph by Herb Greer.

48. A 3,000-year-old wicker basket bottom shows how well even perishable material may be preserved under water if covered quickly by sand or mud. Scraps of broken bronze implements and copper ingots were packed in such baskets on board the Bronze Age shipwreck at Cape Gelidonya.

49. A plastic-cloth balloon, capable of lifting 400 pounds, is filled with air by Frederic Dumas as Claude Duthuit guides the mass of concreted metal cargo to which the balloon is attached. Balloons provided the most effective means of raising heavy objects from the sea-bed at Cape Gelidonya. Photograph by Peter Throckmorton.

50. Bass, Duthuit, Illing, and Throckmorton fit together masses of concreted cargo just raised from the Bronze Age shipwreck at Cape Gelidonya; the lumps will next be photographed and then cleaned with hammers and chisels. Each lump contained well-preserved copper ingots and bronze implements. The expedition camp was finally flooded out by a south wind which sent waves crashing across the narrow beach on which it was situated. Photograph by Herb Greer.

51. Brushwood dunnage, with bark still well preserved, lay across the remains of hull planks at Cape Gelidonya. Using a sheet of frosted plastic, Yüksel Eğdemir begins to sketch the wood which sank within a century of the time of the Trojan War. White material on wood is all that is left of tin ingots, the earliest ever found. Photograph by Peter Throckmorton.

52. Each amphora in the cargo of the Byzantine shipwreck at Yassi Ada is tagged clearly with lettered plastic labels. Drawing on a sheet of plastic, artist Eric Ryan remains always just above what he wishes to plot through the three metre-square wire grid below him. Photograph by Herb Greer.

53. 120 feet below the surface, Laurence Joline measures the vertical distance between a wire grid and a Byzantine amphora below; weighted metre tapes proved more effective for such measurements than the mere stick seen here. Photograph by Herb Greer.

54. Methods used in the excavation of the Byzantine shipwreck at Yassi Ada, Turkey, by the University Museum of the University of Pennsylvania. The anchored barge holds air compressors, electric generator, reserve air tanks, and a one-man Galeazzi recompression

chamber (purchased after the only case of 'the bends' suffered in more than 5,000 dives on the site). Hose tenders on the barge care for the two divers using hookah or narghile hoses. One aqualung diver decompresses 10 feet below the barge, while another checks the catch-bag hanging below the wire basket on top of the air lift; the air-lift tube is supported by an air-filled oil drum welded to its top, and is anchored to two rock-filled oil drums near the wreck. A narghile diver holds to a balloon which carries the lifting basket to the surface. On the wreck itself, one diver operates the air lift, while another takes a photograph through the grid on the base of one of the two photographic towers; the scaffolding of angle iron, in the form of nine large steps, supports the towers. Plane tables are seen on either side of the wreck, with a vertical ranging pole for surveying standing at the upper end of the site. In the actual operation, divers would normally be working in pairs and staying quite close to one another for safety; and it would not be possible to guide the balloon, which quickly increases its speed, so far above the sea-bed. Painting by Pierre Mion. Courtesy National Geographic Society © National Geographic Society.

55. The concretion which had covered one of the eleven iron anchors at Yassi Ada is cleared of sand before being raised to the surface. No iron remains inside the concretion, which has formed a mould of the original anchor. Photo by Jack Sofield.

56. Using an electric lapidary saw, Önder Seren cuts the concretion seen in Plate 55. The mushy iron oxide will be washed out of the concretion, leaving a mould which may be cast with rubber after the sections of concretion are fitted back together. Photograph by Donald Rosencrantz.

57. Eight of the twenty oil lamps found at Yassi Ada give some indication of the quantity and state of preservation of well-dated artifacts which will be found in most shipwrecks. Photograph by Waldemar Illing.

58, 60, 61. Using a photograph of wooden remains taken under water (Plate 58), Frederick van Doorninck pieces together (Plate 60) the fragments to form the plank seen in Plate 61. Photographs by Donald Rosencrantz.

59. Walking up the slope at Yassi Ada from a depth of 120 feet, four divers carry a wire basket containing fragile wooden planks from the Byzantine hull; the black lifting-balloon aids them by relieving some of the weight. Photograph by Mustafa Kapkin.

62. A diver swims up into a submersible decompression chamber after working nearly 140 feet deep on a Roman shipwreck at Yassi

Ada, Turkey. The air-filled sphere holds three divers in comfort; its depth beneath the waves is adjusted by cables and a pulley system below. Air hose and telephone line run to land about fifty yards away. Photograph by John Cassils.

INDEX

Adirondack Museum, 54

aerial photographs and surveys, 30, 35, 82

air lift, 27, 58, 60, 69, 116–24, 134, 147, 152, 148–9, 172, 174

Albenga, 29, 115

Albright, Alan, 144

amateurs, 15–16, 31, 36, 39, 53, 123, 151

Amatitlan, Lake, 39–40, 168

American Civil War: see Cairo

American Colonial period: see bateaux, Chapelle, Olsen, S., *Philadelphia, Royal Savage,* voyageurs, York River

American Indians, 31, 34, 35, 39, 53

anchors, 50, 80, 96, 114, 136, 140, 170, 174

Antalya, Bay of, 81

Antikythera, 29, 74–7, 169

Apollonia, 82–3

Aras, Kemal, 44–6

Artemision, Cape, 29, 72, 169

Asherah, 48, 106–9, 146, 155 171, 172

balloons: see raising methods

Baltic Sea, 42, 60, 168

Barnier, Georges, 142

Bartell, Frank, 48

Basswood Rapids, 36

bateaux, 54, 144

Bean, George, 44, 76

Bearss, Edwin C., 57, 58

Benakis, Alexander, 72

'bends': see diving hazards

Benoît, Fernand, 124

Béziers, 81

Bisso, W. J., 58

Bodrum, 45, 76, 135; Museum, 45, 77

Boëthos, 78

Bond, George, 153

Bouscaras, A., 81

Brill, Robert, 114–15

British Sub-Aqua Club, 31–4

Bronze Age, 47, 80–81, 111, 113, 118; see also Gelidonya, Cape

buoys: see mapping techniques

Byzantine: see Yassi Ada

Caesarea, 83, 84, 117–18

Cairo, 42, 56–8, 124, 167, 168

California, 34–5, 124

Cambridge University, 82–3

Cambser, Lake, 86

canoes, 36, 38, 53, 113, 118

Caribbean, 31, 96

Carpenter, Rhys, 74

CEDAM (Exploration and Water Sports Club of Mexico), 69

Cederlund, C. O., 61

cenote, 64–71, 168–9

chamber and bell, diving, 28–9, 49, 60, 115, 147–50, 154, 174

Champlain, Lake, 54–6

Champréveyres, 118
Chapala, Lake, 41
Chapelle, Howard, 44
Charnay, Désiré, 67
Cherchel, 83
Chersonesos, 83
Chicago, University of, 84
Chichen Itza, 65–9, 117–18, 168–9
cleaning remains, 52, 76, 126, 135; see also cleaning of site under mapping techniques
Cochran, Drayton, 46–7
coffer dam, 52–3, 168
coins, 61, 120, 136
Columbus, 42
communications under water, 28, 107, 115, 142, 148, 170–71
concretion, 124–6, 142–3, 145, 151, 172–4
core samplers, 30, 35, 42–3, 84, 124, 172
Corning Museum of Glass, 114
Council of Underwater Archaeology, 31, 125, 159
Cousteau, Jacques-Yves, 22, 79, 153
Cowen, J. D., 80
Crumlin-Pedersen, Ole, 53
currents: see diving hazards

Davis, E. W., 36, 167
de Borhegyi, Stephan, 17, 39–40, 168
decompression, 25–6, 135–6, 142, 147, 174
decompression sickness: see 'bends' under diving hazards
Demeter, bronze bust of, 44, 47–8, 76–7, 169
Denmark, 52–3

Deutsche Akademie der Wissenschaft, Berlin, 86
Diolé, Philippe, 83
Dioscuria, 84
Divanli, Rasim, 44
diving equipment, 21, 29, 152–3; aqualung, 15–16, 22–3, 70 and passim; helium/oxygen, 48; helmet, 21–2, 45, 50, 53, 55, 167; hookah, 24, 135, 142, 167, 174; narghile: see hookah; oxygen-rebreather, 24; scuba, 23–4 and passim; see also chambers, houses, and submarines
diving hazards: 'bends', 25–6, 28–9, 45, 70, 75, 135–6, 152–4; embolism, 27, 72, 150; currents, 20, 36, 52, 58, 100, 125–6; nitrogen narcosis, 24–5, 152; sharks, 20, 24
diving safety measures, 26, 135, 142, 150, 156
documentary evidence of sites, 30, 36, 38–9, 42–3, 57, 65–6, 86, 114, 151
draining operations, 50–52, 111, 113
Dramont, Cape, 113, 123, 132
dredging, 35, 67, 74, 85; see also grabs
Dumas, Frederic, 96–7, 119–20, 121, 125–6, 131–3, 158, 173
Duthuit, Claude, 120, 150, 169, 172–3
Dzibilchaltun, 29, 70–71

Edgerton, Harold, 42
Edwards, G. Roger, 75
Eğdemir, Yüksel, 78, 109, 138, 150, 173

Eleusis, 80
El Salvador, 41
embolism: see diving hazards

Finike, 45; see also Gelidonya
Flemming, Nicholas, 82
Florida, 63, 70
Fortuna, bronze figurine of, 47–8, 80
Franzén, Anders, 42–3, 60
freshwater sites, 70; see also cenote, lakes, rivers

Gagnan, Emile, 22
Galli Islands, 25, 170
Gargalo, Piero, 88
Gelidonya, Cape, 17, 81, 120, 123–32, 150, 151, 155, 167, 169, 172–3
George, Lake, 53, 144
Germany, 86–7
Gluria, Emilio, 50
Grabau, Warren, 57
grabs, 35, 67–8, 113–15
Grace, Virginia, 46
Grand Congloué, 29, 89, 116–18, 120, 121, 123–4
Greece, National Museum of, 74–6
grids: see mapping techniques
Guatemala, 39, 41–2
Guija, Lake, 41

Haag, Willy, 118, 123
Hagglund, L. F., 55–6
harbours: see Apollonia, Caesarea, Cherchel, Chersonesos, Heleies, Kenchreai, Motya, Sidon, Tyre
Hart, James, 57
Hawkes, C. F. C., 80
Heleies, 84

Helike, 84
Hellenic Federation of Underwater Activities, 90, 170
Hellenistic finds, 45, 76–9
Holland, 52, 109
hookah: see diving equipment
Horsetail Rapids, 36, 38, 117
houses, underwater, 49, 153–4
Huelva, 80
Huston, John, 125

Illing, Waldemar, 172–3
Indiana, University of, 84
Institute of Archaeology, London University, 84, 125
Inverarity, Robert B., 54, 144
Iron Age, 81, 111, 113, 155
iron replacement process, 142–3, 145
Israel, 81, 83, 84, 117
Ivanoff lens, 105, 172
Ixpaco, Lake, 41–2
Izmir Museum, 44, 76

Jacks, M. D., 57
Jamaica, 13, 43, 85, 169–70
Jewell, Donald P., 34–5, 124
Joline, Laurence T., 26, 48, 135–6, 143, 150, 173

Kalamis, 72
Kapitän, Gerhard, 86
Kapkin, Mustafa, 44–7, 77, 132
Kartelias, Nikos, 93, 170
Katzev, Michael, 143, 146, 148
Keller, Ferdinand, 111–13
Keller, Hannes, 152–3
Kenchreai, 84
Kondos, Demetrios, 75
Kreusis, 79
Kyme, 81
Kyrenia, 29, 146, 148

lake dwellings, 52, 86–7, 110–13

lakes, 34–5, 111, 113; see also
Amatitlan, Cambser, Champlain, Chapala, George, Guija, Ixpaco, Nemi, Neuchâtel, Werbellin

Lamboglia, Nino, 100, 115

lamps, 76, 78, 127, 130, 136, 174

Le Tène, 113

Lea, River, 80

Leenhardt, Olivier, 84

Linder, Elisha, 84

Link, Edwin A., 85, 117, 153–4, 170, 172

Link, Marion, 85, 172

Lippold, George, 74

Littlehales, Bates, 70

Livorno, 79

London University: see Institute of Archaeology

Lothrop, S. K., 69

Louvre, 71

Love, Robert, 95–6, 170

Lysippos, 74, 75

magnetometer and magnetic detectors, 30–31, 47, 57, 148, 151

Mahdia, 77–9, 119–20, 123

Mahler, Joy, 68

mapping techniques: buoys, 35, 57, 82, 85–6; cleaning of site, 86–7, 97, 133; drawing under water, 52, 83, 87, 125, 133, 173; elevation measurements, 94–9, 101–2, 105, 133, 170–71, 173; frames, 96–7, 100, 133; grids, 38, 86–7, 97, 100–102, 133, 173–4; photogrammetry, 82, 104–9, 148, 152, 170–72; photomosaics, 99–100, 102–3, 125; plane tables, 97, 133, 170, 174;

tagging, 97, 133, 173; triangulation on surface, 35, 82–3; triangulation under water, 89

Marathon Bay, bronze youth from, 74, 169

Marden, Luis, 69–70

Mariners' Museum, Newport News, Virginia, 114

Marsden, Peter, 53

Marx, Bob, 42

materials found under water: bone, 35, 39, 42, 61, 69–70, 87, 118, 127; brass, 36, 85, 167; brick, 50; bronze, 20, 46, 50–51, 71–5, 77–8, 79–81, 127; cloth, 20, 38, 61, 68–9, 110; copper, 20, 36, 50, 61, 68, 81, 85, 127, 136, 138; glass, 13, 42, 45, 57, 63, 76, 85, 93, 114–15, 120, 139; gold, 20, 66–9, 76, 136; granite, 90–93; iron, 38, 57, 61–2, 85, 136, 143, 174; ivory, 84; lead, 20, 38, 51, 138; leather, 61; marble, 50–51, 73–4, 75, 78, 79; mosaics, 50–51, 84; pewter, 55–6, 85, 114; pottery, 13, 39, 42, 69–70, 76, 78, 80, 85, 115, 136–7; silver, 86, 138; stone other than granite and marble, 35, 38, 39, 42, 50, 60, 110, 127, 138; tin, 129; wood, 20, 42, 43, 50–53, 55, 57–8, 69, 71, 72, 74, 77, 84, 85, 110, 115, 139

Maya artifacts, 39–42, 64–71, 73, 168–9

medieval finds, 34, 46, 86–8

Merifield, Paul, 95

Merlin, Alfred, 79

metal detector, 124, 148, 151, 167, 172

Methone, 99, 170; *see also* Spitha
Mexico, 41, 64, 69
Milwaukee Public Museum, 39
Minnesota Historical Society, 36, 39, 54, 118, 167
Monaco, 80, 84
Motya, 84
museums: *see* Adirondack, Bodrum, Corning, Greece, Izmir, Louvre, Mariners', Milwaukee, Peabody, Royal Ontario, Smithsonian, University, Vatican; Bardo, 77; Florence, 79; Minnesota Historical Society, 39; Monaco, 84; Nemi, 52; Vasa, 61; Vicksburg, 58

Nahe, River, 80
narghile: see diving equipment
National Geographic Society, 36, 47, 69, 85, 105, 132, 146, 169–70, 171
National Museum, Washington: *see* Smithsonian Institution
National Science Federation, 105, 171
Negro youth of bronze, 47–8, 80, 169
Nemi, Lake, 49–52, 168, 170
Neptun Salvage Company, 60, 168
Neuchâtel, Lake, 113, 118
nitrogen narcosis: *see* diving hazards

Olsen, Olaf, 52
Olsen, Stanley J., 63
Owen, David, 135
oxygen, 147, 150
oxygen-rebreather: *see* diving equipment

Parks, Ken, 57

Peabody Museum, Harvard University, 68–9
Pennsylvania, University of: *see* University Museum
Peterson, Mendel, 96, 170
Pheidias, 73
Philadelphia, 55–6
photogrammetry: *see* mapping techniques
photography, underwater, 28, 82, 87, 90, 99–100, 101–5, 125, 158
pile dwellings: *see* lake dwellings
Piombino Apollo, 71–2, 169
Piraeus, 74, 79
plotting devices: *see* mapping techniques
Poidebard, Père, 82–3
polyethylene glycol, 53, 144
pontoons: *see* raising methods
Populonia, 71
Port Royal, 13, 42, 85, 115, 117–18, 169–70, 172
Poulsen, Vagn, 74
Praxiteles, 74, 169
prehistoric finds, 31, 111, 113; *see also* Bronze Age, Iron Age, American Indians
preservation: *see* iron replacement process *and* wood, conservation of
Price, Derek, 76
proton magnetometer: *see* magnetometer

radiocarbon dating, 129
raising methods, 60, 75, 143; with balloons, 54, 126, 135, 173–4; with drums, 54, 56; with pontoons, 58, 60; with winches, 49, 58, 126
ram, ship's, 80

Rebikoff, Dimitri, 104
recompression chamber, 26–7, 70, 135–6, 142, 150, 167, 173–4
refraction, problems of, 23, 28, 101–2, 105, 109, 171
reporting of discoveries, 31
Rhine, River, 80
Rhodes, 79
Ridgway, Brunilde, 72
rivers: see Basswood Rapids, Horsetail Rapids, Lea, Nahe, Rhine, St Marks, Saône, Scheldt, Seine, Thames, Weser, Yazoo, York
Roghi, Gianni, 100
Roman sites, 45, 49–52, 53, 73–5, 77, 88–9, 93, 113, 115, 119, 146–9, 167
Romero, Pablo Bush, 69
Rosencrantz, Donald, 48, 95, 104, 109, 170–71
Roskilde Fjord, 52–3, 168
Royal Ontario Museum, 36
Royal Savage, 54–5
Ryan, Eric, 150, 171, 173

St Marks River, 63–4
Sanders, John 42
Santamaria, Claude, 119
Saône, River, 80
sarcophagi, 80, 93–4, 146, 170
Sardinia, 100
Scheldt, River, 80
Schwab, Friedrich, 113
Scripps Institution of Oceanography, 48
scuba: see diving equipment
sculpture, 49, 62, 71–80, 84, 167–9
Seine, River, 80
shipwrecks investigated or excavated: see Albenga, Antiky-
thera, Artemision, *Cairo*, Dramont, Gelidonya, Grand Congloué, Kyrenia, Mahdia, Marsden, Methone, Nemi, *Philadelphia*, Roskilde Fjord, *Royal Savage*, Spargi, Taranto, Titan, *Vasa*, York River
shipwrecks, causes: enemy bombardment, 55, 114; fire, 55, 74; formation of blockades, 52, 114; mine, 56; reefs, 46, 87–8; wind, 43
Sicily, 71, 84, 88
Sidon, 83
Sivirine, A., 119–20
Skerrett, Robert, 55
Smithsonian Institution, 44, 56, 59, 96, 144, 170
sonic devices, 42, 78, 85, 151–2
Spanish galleons, 31, 144
Spargi, 100–101, 123
Spitha, Cape, 89–94
sponge divers and draggers, 21, 44–7, 68, 72–5, 76–9, 81, 119, 139, 151–2, 167
staff, excavation, 16–17, 26–7, 29, 82–3, 123, 132, 140–42, 147, 150, 156–7
stereophotography, 82, 104–5, 109, 148, 152, 171–2
Stockholm Harbour, 42, 60
stratigraphy, 63, 69, 87, 111, 118, 124
submarines, 28–9, 48–9, 106–9, 146, 152–4, 171
submersible decompression chamber, 147–50, 157, 177
suction hoses, 52; see also air lift
Sukhumi Bay, 84
surface, observation from, 55, 82, 86, 111–14

wedish Navy, 43, 60
witzerland, 52, 86, 110–13, 117

ailliez, Philippe, 79, 99, 123
aranto, 93, 146
aylor, Joan du Plat, 84, 125, 129
elephone booth, underwater, 148, 170
elevision, 28, 47–9, 54, 77, 151
hames, River, 33–4, 53, 80
hompson, Edward H., 67–9
hrockmorton, Peter, 44–6, 77, 89–94, 125–6, 132, 146, 173
itan (Ile du Levant), 99, 123, 172
öpke, Manfred, 39, 168
wns and settlements under water : see California, Cambser, Champréveyres, Dioscuria, Heleies, Helike, lake dwellings, Port Royal, Werbellin
wns and settlements under water, causes: dams, 15, 34; earthquakes, 15, 84–5; fire, 87; possible change of sea level, 15, 83
owvane, 47
ozzer, Alfred M., 68
aining, 16, 26–7, 53, 156–7
reileben, Hans Albrekt von, 60
ulane University, 69
unisian Antiquities Department, 79
unisian Club of Underseas Studies, 79, 119
yre, 82–3

nderwater archaeology : definition of, 13, 18, 53; comparison with land archaeology, 15, 18, 20–21, 27, 29–31, 35, 63, 82, 110, 115–16, 132; cost of, 17, 76, 147–8, 154–5

U.S. National Park Service, 57, 59
U.S. Navy, 58, 70, 153, 158
University Museum of University of Pennsylvania, 30, 47, 75, 77, 95, 97, 100, 104, 105, 120, 125, 132, 146, 152, 167, 170–71

Valcour Island, 55
van Doorninck, Frederick, 135, 143, 145–6, 174
Vasa, 42–3, 60–62, 124, 144, 155, 167–8
Vatican Museum, 50
Vicksburg, Mississippi, 56, 59–60
Vikings, 52, 168
visibility under water, 20, 23, 28, 52, 60, 89, 90, 98–9, 102–4, 151
voyageurs, 35–6, 118, 167

Ward-Perkins, John, 94
water jets, 52, 57–60, 124, 147
Waterman, Stanton, 46
Werbellin, Lake, 86
Weser, River, 80
Wheeler, Robert C., 36, 118, 167
Whittlesey, Julian, 104, 171
wood, conservation of, 51, 53, 144
wood, state of preservation under water, 43, 45, 50, 52–4, 57–8, 60, 61, 68, 85–6, 126, 144, 172–4
Woolworth, Alan 39

X-ray, 85

Yassi Ada, 16–17, 26–7, 29, 45–6, 87, 95, 97, 99, 100, 103–5, 120, 132–50, 170–71, 173–9
Yazoo River, 56–7, 167, 168
York River, 114, 115

Zetterström nozzle, 60

MORE ABOUT PENGUINS
AND PELICANS

THE HITTITES

O. R. Gurney

The Hittites as a legendary Palestinian tribe are familiar
to us from our schooldays. In this book the story is told
of the rediscovery of the historical Hittites during the
last eighty years, as the result of excavation and the
decipherment of cuneiform and hieroglyphic documents.
The Hittites of history were a great nation of Asia
Minor, whose kings treated on equal terms with those
of Egypt, Babylon, and Assyria, during a period of about
two hundred years in the second millennium B.C.
There was an Indo-European strain in them which is
revealed in their language and perhaps in the physical
types of some of the Hittite prisoners represented on
Egyptian monuments. Their earliest social organization
also shows some points of resemblance to that of the
heroic age of Greece. Their religion on the other hand
seems to have been largely that of the indigenous
population, who must be supposed to have inhabited
the country before the Indo-European reached it. They
developed a rupestrian art, which has its roots in the
soil of Mesopotamia, but exhibits a strong and
independent style of its own.

This is an attempt to present a balanced picture of what
is known of the Hittites and in the chapter on literature
to give some impression of the more important types
of documents found among their archives.

THE PYRAMIDS OF EGYPT

I. E. S. Edwards

When *The Pyramids of Egypt* was first published – as a Pelican – in 1947, it was immediately recognized as a work of real importance in the field of Egyptology. Since then many new facts have been unearthed and recorded.

In this new edition the author, who is Keeper of Egyptian Antiquities at the British Museum, has completely revised his text and incorporated the latest knowledge. He presents us with the most up-to-the-minute answer to that eternal question : 'How and why did the ancient Kings of Egypt build their gigantic geometrical monuments?' For today it is possible to trace their early history with some exactitude and to follow the gradual evolution from the simple pre-dynastic tomb to the Step Pyramid of Zoser.

A very comprehensive bibliography of the greatly increased literature on the Pyramids is included, and many new line-drawings and half-tone illustrations have been added.

THE VIKINGS

Johannes Brønsted

Professor Brønsted's purpose is to shed light upon the Nordic Viking, that strange phenomenon of European history from A.D. 800 to 1100. He analyses the motives of the Viking raids and voyages, and investigates the reasons why the Vikings could occupy the North Atlantic islands but could not secure their settlements in North America; why they were able to reach all the coast of Western Europe and penetrate Eastern Europe to Istanbul and Baghdad but could not penetrate Central Europe. The Vikings' acceptance of Christianity, a religion quite alien to their own philosophy, is also considered.

The book, now re-issued in a revised translation, deals also with the background and origin of the Vikings, their industries and equipment, ships and armies, social organization and daily life, ideas and beliefs as they are reflected in runic inscriptions, burial customs, and Icelandic medieval literature.